D1696111

Rebecca Jo Slayden-McMahan is a writer and teacher. She had a teaching career in Clarksville, Montgomery County and at Austin Peay State University in Clarksville, Tennessee. She was a classroom middle grades teacher of science and social studies for six years. She has been a teacher at Austin Peay State University for forty-four years. She is an avid sailor and owns a 33.5' hunter sailboat which is moored at Portman Marina on Lake Hartwell in Anderson S.C. She has two sons, Jonathan and Christopher McMahan, who live in Anderson. She enjoys storytelling and the interesting and whimsical nature of the written word.

This work is dedicated to five generations of my family.

Rebecca Jo Slayden-McMahan

Grinnin' Like a Jenny Eatin' Saw Briars

AUSTIN MACAULEY PUBLISHERS™

LONDON * CAMBRIDGE * NEW YORK * SHARJAH

Ordering Information
Quantity sales: Special discounts are available on quantity purchases by corporations, associations, and others. For details, contact the publisher at the address below.

Publisher's Cataloging-in-Publication data
Slayden-McMahan, Rebecca Jo
Grinnin' Like a Jenny Eatin' Saw Briars

ISBN 9781638292487 (Paperback)
ISBN 9781638292494 (Hardback)
ISBN 9781638292500 (ePub e-book)

Library of Congress Control Number: 2022907880

www.austinmacauley.com/us

First Published 2022
Austin Macauley Publishers LLC
40 Wall Street, 33rd Floor, Suite 3302
New York, NY 10005
USA

mail-usa@austinmacauley.com
+1 (646) 5125767

I would like to thank my family and colleagues for sharing life that is represented by these Southern sayings and stories and my sons, Christopher Steven McMahan and Jonathan Lindsay McMahan, who requested that I write this book. The original art work on the cover of this book was created by artist Jon Duncan of Clarksville, Tennessee.

A Jenny or Female Donkey
Original Art by Jon Duncan of Clarksville, Tennessee

Prologue

I was born in 1950 and grew up in Clarksville, Tennessee. My extended family lived in what we called the "country," meaning that it was a rural area about fifty miles north of Nashville, Tennessee. I am of German, English, and Irish lineage. Over the years I have reflected on our language and the unusual sayings we used in daily conversation and in telling stories. The use of metaphors and similes is put into practice in idioms and colloquial expressions to convey meaning in our rich stories, which carry meaning very much as proverbs. I remember the very first dictionary that I ever owned, *"Webster's Elementary Dictionary: A Dictionary for Boys and Girls,"* published in 1941. It was a warm fall day when we went to town to purchase my dictionary required in my fourth-grade class. I remember holding the most precious book and telling my mother that someday I would know every word between its covers. I have always loved vocabulary and the wonderful feelings and amazing ideas that words can convey. This book contains 2,300 special sayings that I grew up using in everyday communication and interaction. Everyone I knew used these sayings. It was a way of life and reflected our culture.

In 1968 I attended Austin Peay State University in Clarksville, Tennessee, and earned a Bachelor of Science degree in Elementary Education and Biology in 1971. I earned the master's degree in Curriculum and Instruction from Austin Peay State University in 1972. After graduation I taught middle school science for six years. In 1979 I took a position at Austin Peay State University in the College of Education. At this time, I began my doctorate in Curriculum and Instruction and Leadership at Vanderbilt University. I graduated from Vanderbilt University in 1984 with a Doctor of Education degree. During the three-year period of working on my doctorate, I also taught full-time for Austin

Peay State University. Also, during that three-year period, I had two sons who were born fifteen months apart. They are my greatest achievements. I spent 35 years as a professor of teacher education in the College of Education at Austin Peay State University. I served as Chair of the Department of Teaching and Learning in the College of Education for eight years. In 2016 I retired and now work from home in Anderson, South Carolina. My two sons both live in Anderson. My property is ten minutes from Lake Hartwell's Portman Marina, where I moor my 33.5' Hunter sailboat, *Lickety Split.* My boat is Coast Guard-documented so I carry Coast Guard numbers and the title of "Captain Rebecca McMahan".

The following 2,300 idioms or sayings in this book are ones that I grew up hearing from family, extended family, and community members. Throughout a lifetime of education, communication, and conversing, I have come to understand that everyone does not use these unique sayings. For this reason, I have decided to record and share them with others. The sayings that I share came from individuals living within a fifty-mile radius of Clarksville-Montgomery County, Tennessee. I have included true "family" stories entitled "Stories from Then" throughout the book to introduce you to the wonderful family I had while growing up that taught me to interact with this "special language". My Aunt Arlie Wilder used to say that one thing she hated to see was a woman grinning and laughing out loud with her mouth open like a "Jenny Eatin' Saw Briars". For this reason, I choose this title for the book. Hopefully you will find yourself *"Grinnin' Like a Jenny Eatin' Saw Briars"* as you read.

Dr. Rebecca Slayden-McMahan, Author

Clarksville-Montgomery
and Dickson County

The main source of the sayings comes from four generations of family and friends living within a fifty-mile radius in Middle Tennessee.

Format of Book

The book contains some 2,500 sayings, colloquialisms, and idioms. The use of descriptive imagery, common idioms, and sayings such as these convey concise ideas. They are often used in informal conversations. An idiom is a metaphorical figure of speech. Figures of speech go beyond the literal meanings of words. These sayings define us, my family, and those with whom I have interacted as a fifth-generation southern community of people. The sayings in this book have been researched, and it is found that the origins of many come from either the Bible or ancient times. The sayings are specific to a fifty-mile radius of Montgomery and Dickson Counties in Middle Tennessee. They have been defined by me based on the implied meaning that we had in mind when we used them or by definition and origin from multiple sources of the internet. I have included several true stories about my family that will allow the reader to become acquainted with the individuals with whom I interacted with, including three generations of family and friends that used these sayings. The true stories are entitled: "Stories from Then".

Stories from Then:

15

Sayings, Idioms and Colloquialisms
Defined by the Author from Common Knowledge or Research

A [137]

a bad egg in every dozen	every group has its troublemakers
a barefaced lie	a bold obvious falsehood
a bird in the hand is worth two in the bush	a sure thing is worth a promised deal
a bird singing like spring	a zestfully singing bird
a book like an old friend	a thing of comfort that you are used to
a cold check	a check with insufficient funds in the bank
a cold deck	a bad card game
a contended bull won't leave his pen	a person accused will not usually walk away from a confrontation
a cryin' shame	a real shame

a day late and a dollar short	something that is woefully wanting
a Dear John letter	ending a relationship
a dime a dozen	a very cheap item
a dollar waitin' on a dime	I am more important than you and I'm waiting on you
a dyin' cause	a lost cause or something that is hopeless
a face as smooth as a baby's behind	a smooth complexion
a fly in the buttermilk	a problem that arises and prohibits progress
a friend in need is a friend indeed	when people are in need, they tend to call on you
a gut feeling	a real strong feeling
a half a loaf is better than no loaf at all	a little is better than none
a heart cold as ice	an uncaring person
a hoot and a holler	a short distance
a house of ill repute	a house of prostitution
a long row to hoe	a long set of tasks that are difficult and demanding
a man is judged by the company he keeps	people make opinions about you based on others that you befriend or associate with

a man's man — a man admired for traditionally masculine interests

a stitch in time saves nine — it is wise to take action when it is needed, saving yourself a worse situation if you delay

actions speak louder than words — what you do in terms of actions is a better example of your character and behavior than what you just say

all that glitters is not gold — often things are not what they seem

all used up — something is depleted including a person's energy

all wound up — excited and stimulated

a lick and a promise — give a task short attention

My Mother: Ruby Jo Slayden-Slaughter

Story from Then... *"A Lick and a Promise"* by Ruby Jo Slaughter Slayden

My mother's name is Ruby Jo Slaughter Slayden. She was an example of what a mother should be and my role model. She was one of the best homemakers I have ever known. She was creative and thrifty. Her house was always in order and exceptionally clean. She was a stay-at-home mom until my sister, and I went to middle school. At this point she went back to work as an assistant first for a dentist and then an optician. She continued with involvements and support of our schoolwork, church work, direction of the youth and adult choirs at church, and work with girl scouts. Her house still stayed very clean. I was always proud of our home. On the weekends we camped and went boating. In the summers we traveled south to Florida. Her home always stayed very clean. At times she would say I am going to give the house "a lick and a promise", meaning that the cleaning for that week would not be deep cleaning. After all the "outdoors was waiting".

a man's home is his castle	a working man's home is a castle to him
a "Negative Nellie"	a person who always takes a negative viewpoint
a new broom sweeps clean	a new boss or administrator tends to bring in his own people
a person has rabbit ears	they are eavesdropping or hear exceptionally well
a place time forgot	an old place once occupied that is no longer inhabited or is abandoned
a pretty penny	a lot of money
a rabbit just ran across my grave	indicated when a person shivers for no reason
a ravelin'	a string or thread on your clothes
a real lemon	something you buy that is defective
a rollin' stone gathers no moss	if you stay busy, you stay informed
a rovin' eye	someone is looking around for a lover
a runnin' loan	money that is borrowed on long term or occasionally

a shot in the dark	a best guess or estimate that you can't be sure of
a slice short of a pie	someone who is mentally impaired
a smokin' gun case	police solve a crime by finding a person with a gun in their hand which has just been fired or a case solved easily and immediately
a sneakin' suspicion	a pretty good clue
a snow knee deep to Jim Hord	an extreme snow in deep drifts
a stitch in time saves nine	prevention is better than correction
a stone's throw away	a very short distance
a stool pigeon	an informer or snitch
a strang' danglin'	a string on a person's clothes which is a stray string
a sucker is born every minute	there are many gullible people in this world
a tough nut to crack	a hard thing to figure out or to understand
a two-holer	an outdoor toilet with two seats
a watch pot never boils	patience is required while cooking
a word to the wise	a piece of advice that a prudent or wise person would follow
a whale of a catch	a large catch
a Yankee dime	a kiss
about half-cracked	half crazy
about time to bed down	about time to go to sleep

about to bust a gut	mad enough to explode or can also mean engorged from over eating
about to crack up	very emotionally distraught
above board	above reproach
absence makes the heart grow fonder	when individuals are not together, they learn to appreciate each other's company more
ace in the hold	a sure thing
achin' for a shakin'	just asking for and deserving trouble
achin' for you	missing you or desiring you
actin' a fool	acting foolish
actin' like she's somebody	acting arrogant and pious
actin' like two love birds	demonstrating affection openly and inappropriately in public
actin' out	acting poorly in a social situation
adding insult to injury	saying something to just make things worse
afraid he will rat on me	afraid he will tell on me
ah...go shake a bush	get lost
ain't got the sense you were born with	acting senseless, immature, or dumb
ain't worth a dime	worthless
airin' out dirty linen	talking about personal issues or political issues in an inappropriate way to inappropriate audiences
all bark and no bite	false front in actions in threatening manner
all cooped up	too confined

all dolled up	dressed up
all dressed up and nowhere to go	overdressed for the occasion
all fagged out	tired to the point of exhaustion
all liquored up	drunk or intoxicated
all puckered up	lips ready to be kissed
all shook up	emotionally distraught
all stopped up	a sinus blockage
all thumbs	clumsy and lacking manual dexterity
all tied up	busy
all torn up	upset emotionally
all tuckered out	physically exhausted
all washed out	physically exhausted
all washed up	behind the times or out of date and unpopular
all wool and a yard wide	description meaning a person is a real fine person
all worked up	emotionally upset more so than a situation should warrant
all wound up	very excited and possessing almost uncontrollable energy
all wrapped up in himself	very self-centered
always gotta put your two cents in	always offering an opinion whether it is welcomed or not
always had to suck a hind tit	always had to give way to the needs or demands of others reaping negative consequences as a result
always kickin' about somethin'	always complaining
always lookin' over my shoulder	constantly being

	concerned about negative consequences you might reap due to inappropriate past actions on your part with others
always rockin' the boat	always causing trouble
always slinging mud	always talking about someone in a negative way
an ax to grind	a personal agenda one wishes to accomplish
an old sour puss	a very disgruntled person
an ounce of prevention is worth a pound of cure	preventive action is preferable to remedial action
apple a day keeps the doctor away	fruit is good for the digestion and health and prevents illness
apple of my eye	my favorite
April showers bring May flowers	"rain" often seen as a negative occurrence is responsible to something very beautiful and positive in the long run
are you upset	are you in emotionally distress
aren't in their right mind	are not thinking clearly or rationally
argue with a fence post	someone who is extremely argumentative with anyone about anything
arms like a blacksmith	extremely muscular
army brat	offspring of a military-connected parent
as busy as a one-armed paper hanger	busy with limited resources or help
as cute as a pig	very attractive

as easy as takin' candy from a baby	a simple task
as honest as the day is long	completely honest all the time
as luck would have it	as it would happen due to misfortune
as old as the hills	geology dates the "hills" as ancient as time itself
as red as the fresh spanked baby	pink in color
as rung out as a dishrag	tired to the point of exhaustion
as set in your ways as an old maid	inflexible
as slow as the seven-year itch	very slow
as sure-footed as a donkey	very stable on one's feet
as the crow flies	in a straight line
as thick as fleas	very thickly infested or crowded
as useless as a one-handled wheelbarrow	without functional utility
as useless as a one-legged man	not only nonfunctional but totally inefficient, ineffective, and humorous
in a tail kickin' contest	
asking for trouble	putting yourself the situation that you know is potentially problematic
asking papa for her hand	requesting paternal permission to marry
at a snail's pace	very, very slowly
at loose ends	between jobs, bored or without direction
at the crossroads of life	come to the place where you must decide which will significantly affect the destiny and direction of your life
at the drop of a hat	immediately

at your jumpin' off point	at the point of giving up
aw shucks	saying this indicates embarrassment

B [166]

back breakin' labor	hard manual work
back pocket money man	someone who has paper bills of currency
backseat driver	a passenger prompting the driver
backstabber	a sneaky, non-physically dangerous person
back to the salt mine	back to work
bad luck comes in threes	it seems that three different unfortunate or bad things always happen to a person at the same time
bad egg	a bad person
bad news	a problematic person
bad seed	a second-generation troublemaker or bad person resembling his parent who was a troublemaker
bad to the bone	completely bad
baker's dozen	thirteen
bald as a cue ball	completely bald as a billiard ball
bald as an eagle	no hair or fur
bald as an egg	totally bald
bald-faced lie	This means a lie told without concern for the ethical implications in disregard for those who will be affected. It involves

	ignoring clear and plain information and is unmistakably inaccurate.
ballin' the jack	A locomotive at full speed

Story from Then... *"Ballin' the Jack"* Gertrude Clarice Robbins Slaughter

My maternal grandmother, Gertrude Clarice Robbins Slaughter, was the first female railroad agent for the Tennessee Central Railroad in Clarksville, Tennessee. She used the term "Ballin' the Jack", which means that a train is speeding down the track at full speed while making excellent time in relation to schedule by "going at full speed". She went to college and achieved a degree in business when women as a rule did not go to college. As a railroad agent, first in St. Bethlehem, Tennessee, and then Clarksville, Tennessee, she managed the station in what was then a "man's world". I traveled with her at times when she served as a relief operator in Baxter or Lebanon, Tennessee. At train station she used a telegraph for messages rather than a telephone. She also had a telegraph system in her home to allow her to talk with my grandfather in his shop downstairs like a modern-day intercom. There was a large hoop that looked like a large tennis racket with two wires running through the middle of it. She would attach a typed message to the hoop and hold it up to the engineer of the train. He would take the message off and drop the hoop. It was my job to run down the track and retrieve the hoop after the train passed.

Railroad: Gertrude Robbins Slaughter

Tennessee Central Trains

banana short of a bunch   not mentally sound

barbers shop   a shop that cuts men's hair
                                  primarily

Artifacts found in ancient Egyptian tombs date to 6,000 years ago. During the Middle Ages barbers not only cut hair but performed surgery. In 1745 a bill was passed in England separating barbers from surgeons. Barbers kept the red and white pole as a symbol of a time when they performed simple surgery and pulled teeth. (Barbering Time Line, 2021)

Story from Then: *"Barber Shop"* ...Arlie Mae Baker Wilder

In the 1920s men went to barber shops and women went to beauty shops. It was unheard of for a man to enter a beauty shop. Some women did go to the regular barber especially in small towns where beauty shops weren't as available or more costly. My great Aunt Arlie was not the norm. My great uncle, Claude Wilder, operated a barber shop in Eustis, Florida. This is where he met Arlie Mae Baker, my great aunt. This was an unusual situation because in the 1930s, the patronage of a barbershop was almost exclusively male. Taking one look at Arlie, he told one of the male patrons, "That is the woman that I am going to marry." This was truly a case of love at first sight.

My Great Uncle Claude and Great Aunt Arlie May Baker Wilder

barefoot and pregnant an old saying indicating that a woman's place is in the home, and she serves the major purpose of producing the next generation

barely holdin' on	almost to the point of giving up or seeing a situation as hopeless
barely keepin' your nose out of water	almost financially destroyed
barely treading water	barely able to meet one's financial obligations
barking up the wrong tree	accusing the wrong person or party or assuming something that is incorrect or not true
barn raisin'	The building of a barn was usually accomplished within forty-eight hours in the south because every relative and neighbor within a twenty-mile radius came to help. The men worked on the barn and the women cooked meals.
Bas-ack-wards	backwards
bats in his belfry	mentally ill or crazy
batty	crazy or mentally ill
bawled out	verbally assaulted
be that as it may	regardless
beads of sweat	perspiring profusely
beanpole	thin person
beat around the bush	discussing an issue without coming to the direct point
beat him to the draw	arrive at something first
beatin' a dead horse	going over and over an issue which has been previously and clearly stated

beatin' the devil around a bush	mincing words or hesitating
beauty is skin-deep	a person's physical appearance cannot describe their character, personality, attitude, wisdom, or talents
beauty shop	a predominantly female hair care establishment
been around a long time	experienced
been around the block	has a lot of common sense through experience as well as formal education
been there, done that	I have previously experienced what you are talking about
Beer-barreled	an enlarged abdomen or an obese person
beet red	pink in color
behind bars	in jail
behind the eight ball	you are in big trouble
behind the times	out of style
beside herself	unable to reason
best end of the bargain	a very good deal
better late than never	a task accomplished after the due date, or something done untimely
better pull your chestnuts the fire	a warning to stop an out of action
better quit while you're ahead	don't try to accomplish too much at one time
better to be tried by twelve than to be carried by six	a legal litigation may be disturbing and damaging but the situation could be worse in the fact that you

33

	could be the victim of fatal violence
between a rock and a hard place	in a difficult situation
beyond measure	so valuable that it is deemed priceless
Bible thumper	a person who is always quoting the Bible in a condescending way to others
bidin' your time	waiting patiently
big-boned	a large, framed person
big enough to go bear huntin' with a broomstick	a person of large stature
big fish in a little pond	an important individual socially or politically in a small and isolated geographic area or situation
big mouth	a person who talks too much
Big Sandy	Big Sandy is the small town in Benton County Tennessee that my Great Grandmother Mattie Robbins came from. She is the mother of Gertrude Robbins Slaughter, who is my maternal grandmother.

(Left) Mattie Robbins and Gertrude Clarice Robbins Slaughter (Right). Gertrude's grandfather and Mattie's father was William Henderson Robbins.

William was the last surviving Confederate soldier in Benton County and last surviving soldier on either side of the great conflict. He served with the Wilson Calvary Company of the Napier Division of the Confederate Army during the Civil War.

Note: For more information on William Henderson Robbins, see the saying:

"Jump-Jig" p. 79 *William Henderson Robbins*

big wig	an important individual
bigger than life	very real
bird brain	an individual with limited cognitive ability due to no mental deficiency
birds of a feather will flock together	people tend to seek out others like themselves
birthday suit	in a naked or unclothed state
bitin' of the hand that feeds him	turning against your support
bitin' the bullet	making the best of a situation
bitter as quinine	extremely bitter and a medication used to treat malaria
black as pitch	extremely black or dark
black as the ace of spades	extremely black or dark
Black Draught	a laxative used in the 1900s
blast	exclamation of disgust
blazin' a trail	attempting to move forward without direction or previous experience

bleedin' like a stuck hog	bleeding profusely compared to a hog at slaughter
Bless Pat	saying of exclamation and surprise in a positive way
bless your little pea-pickin' heart	Ernie Ford's saying used by everyone as a term of endearment
blew a fuse	got angry and verbally reacted
blew all his money	wasted his money
blind as a bat	visually impaired...though bats really aren't
blind in one eye and can't see out of the other	very visually impaired
blinded by the light	does not see the reality of the situation
blockhead	hardheaded
blood is thicker than water	family members and family relations are cherished and honored over those between individual who are not genetically related
bloodshot	red eyed mostly from drinking or loss of sleep
blow your mind	totally amaze you
blow your nose...you're a big girl now	act your age and take responsibility for your actions
blow your stack	lose your temper
blowin' smoke	being deceitful
blowin' up storm	*meteorological conditions* predict an actual storm, or the social "climate" of a situation indicate an

	approaching negative situation
blowin' your own horn	bragging on yourself
blown out of proportion	something greatly exaggerated
board and keep	paying your part financially in a situation
body like a sack full of doorknobs	a human body which is suffering because of obesity or extra weight gain from both an aesthetic and physical standpoint ultimately from the lack of physical exercise and proper diet
bone bare	poor
bone of contention	an issue which has caused problems
bone-tired	physically tired to the point of exhaustion
bone to pick	problem to be discussed
bony	skinny
boomtown	a community undergoing rapid growth due to sudden economic shock
boondoggle	something that is a waste of time
Bottled up	hold in your feelings
bootlickin'	attempting to align someone with yourself through disrespectable means
bored to tears	extremely bored
born loser	an unsuccessful individual
born with a silver spoon in his mouth	born into a wealthy family
bosom buddy	best friend

bottom line	a limit of tolerance
bottom of the barrel	a last choice
bought it sight unseen	a purchase without review
bouncin' baby boy	a healthy child
'Bout done	almost finished
'Bout ready to turn his toes up	near death

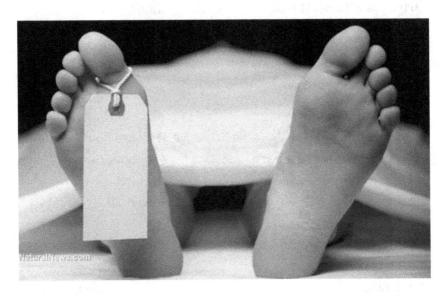

boy is he brazen	behavior, which is risky, rude, and takes inappropriate actions
boy...did her eyes pop out	she was surprised
brayin' like a jackass	laughing loudly
break a leg	good luck
break a sweat	begin to perspire from exertion, especially manual labor
break the spell	change the impending negative circumstances or potential outcome like superstitiously "breaking a bad spell"

breakin' in new shoes	getting used to a new pair of shoes
breedin' like a rabbit	reproducing at a rapid rate
breedin' like flies	reproducing fast
brick shy of a load	mentally incompetent
bright and early	at sunrise
bright as a 15-watt bulb	dumb
bringin' up the caboose	train term which means coming in last because the caboose is the last car on a train
bringin' up the rear	being at the end
broad as it is long	it makes no real difference
broad as the side of a barn	very obese and wide across the hips
broken-hearted	saddened greatly
brown-eyed greedy gut...going around eatin' the world up	a greedy person
brush mouth	untrustworthy in word
buck fever	an inability to shoot an animal once you have it within the sites of the gun
buck up	gather your courage and stand up and "be a man"
buck-naked	no clothes at all
bug eyes	protruding eyes
buildin' castles in the sand	making an investment of time or effort which will not last
built his house on sandy soil	he did not prepare properly
bullheaded	obstinate
bullseye	exactly
bully beef	known as bully beef during WW1 and known today as corned beef. It is made

from finely minced corned beef in gelatin. Bully beef and hardtack biscuits were main field rations during starting in WW1. (Express, 2021)

bumfuzzled	confused
bumpy road	a hard time
bun in the oven	pregnant
buried in his work	completely engrossed in his work
burn your bridges	eliminate your contacts or destroy your network
burned to a crisp	charred
burnin' daylight	waiting late in the morning of the day to start work
burnin' my bridges behind me	severing ties or important communications and relationships
burnin' the candle at both ends	working too hard or too long also doing too many things
burnin' the midnight oil	working late into the evening hours
burnt out	used up or consumed
burns like hell	the ultimate burning
burr in his britches	something bothering him
burr under his saddle	something bothering him
busty	large-breasted
busy as a bee	very occupied
busy body	a nosy person
butter wouldn't melt in her mouth	she is very careful to not offend
butterin' someone up to	flatter someone to gain favor from them in the future

buttin' heads	getting into an argument
buttin' in	intruding
by the book	exactly as prescribed
by the skin of his teeth	barely
C [156]	
cabin fever	tired of staying inside the house especially in cold weather
call it a day	stop or finish what you are doing at the time to resume activity the next day or at a future time
call the sawbones	call the doctor
call up book	take role or when school starts
called home	dead and gone to Heaven
called on the carpet	reprimanded
came out of the woodwork	came into view or action without any warning
came out half-cocked	half-cocked refers to being ill-prepared as a gun was partially cocked
came unglued	lost composure
camera-shy	resisting being photographed
can I help you...I'm just lookin' around	salesclerks in the 1930s always asked you if you needed assistance in shopping
cantankerous	ill-tempered and cranky with a difficult disposition
can't judge a book by its cover	first impressions can be misleading
can't fight himself out of a paper bag	a weakling or person of limited physical stamina

can't fill him up	refers to a person with a voracious appetite
can't find you way out of a cardboard box	weak or defenseless
can't get ahead	cannot make a gain or an advantage
can't get along with women... can't live without them	women give this person trouble
can't get blood from a turnip	if the potential doesn't exist, it cannot be met
can't get cranked up	can't get motivated
can't get fired up	can't get excited or interested in something
can't get started for stopping	cannot get organized
can't get there from here	cannot find my way
can't have your cake and eat it too	must decide what you want and what you are willing to give to gain
can't hear it thunder	deaf
can't keep from laughin'	find something very humorous
can't keep up this pace	cannot keep working at such a hard rate or pace
can't keep up with the times	can't remain current or stylish
can't make a silk purse out of a sow's ear	can't make something out of nothing
can't see for lookin'	not focused
can't see past the end of your nose	nearsighted both figuratively and literally
can't see the fire for the smoke	too close to the situation to be objective

can't see the forest for the trees	looking at the limited view instead of the whole picture
can't stand him	dislike him
can't stand to just sit down	nervous or anxious
can't teach an old dog new tricks	it is hard to break old habits or to learn new things
can't tell what you're sayin'	don't understand you
can't wade in the creek without gettin' your feet wet	if you get involved, you become a part of the process
carryin' on like a couple of school kids	behaving childishly
carryin' the heat	carrying a gun on your person
carved in stone not permanent	
cashed in his chips	died
castor oil	oil from the castor bean which is given as a laxative usually every spring to children for the purpose of purging and cleaning their system
catawampus	askew or lopsided
catch your death of cold	will get deathly sick
catchin' a cold	feeling the first signs of sickness
catchin' twenty winks	taking a nap
cat house	a house of ill-repute or prostitution
caught daydreamin'	distracted or unfocused
caught in the act of	seen while doing something
caught red-handed	guilty of stealing
'Cause a dog chases a Greyhound	

don't mean he wants to ride	sometimes we're curious but don't want to get involved
chain smoker	immediately smoking one cigarette after another
changed horses in the middle of the stream	change your mind
changin' your mind	rethinking a situation
charge it to the dust and let the rain settle it	disavowing responsibility for something
chasin' his own tail	accomplishing nothing
chasin' rainbows	on a fool's mission or an impossible task
chasin' shadows	attempting to accomplish an impossible task
chatterbox	too talkative
cheap as a dollar watch	cheap
chewin' the fat	talking about current events
chickened out	lost nerve
chief cook and bottle washer	in charge of the kitchen and culinary duties
children should be seen and not heard	the opinion that children should be reserved, obedient, and quiet
chip off the old block	like his parent
chivalry	in the early 1900s when a couple married, the friends of the couple would gather at the newlyweds' home on the wedding night and beat on pots and pans and make noise to disturb the couple as a humorous custom
chomping at the bit	very impatient

chow time	time to eat
class A moron	a very stupid person
classy	very attractive
clean as a whistle	completely cleaned
clean up your act	start acting responsibly
cleanliness is next to Godliness	cleanliness is a virtue
clear as can be	very clear
climb the ladder	move through the ranks ascending in importance or rank
clobbered	beaten up in a fight, also drunk
clock-watcher	demonstrating great concern for time or the passage of time
clock work	with precision
close only counts in hand grenades and horseshoes	it must be exact without question about precision
cloud with a silver lining'	a bad circumstance can often end up as an unexpected advantage
Coca-Cola	Coca-Cola syrup was created by Dr. John Stith Pemberton, a local pharmacist in Atlanta, Georgia. The syrup was combined with carbonted water to produce the drink on May 8, 1886.

(Coca-Cola, 2021)

cocklebur Cocklebur plants *(Xanthium strumarium)* produce hundreds of little football-shaped burs, about one inch (2.5 cm) long and covered with stiff, hooked spines. Each cocklebur fruit contains two seeds that may remain viable for many years. The prickly burs hook into your clothing and become tightly attached.

(Britannia, 2021)

cock of the roost	dominate male in a group
cold as can be	extreme cold
cold as kraut	extreme cold
cold enough to freeze the balls off a brass monkey	It is believed that a brass monkey is a tray used for storage of cannonballs. The balls were stored in the tray. Extreme cold weather caused the balls to fall off the tray. (Grammar Monster, 2021)
cold enough to kill hogs	hogs in Tennessee are slaughtered in November usually at Thanksgiving time when the weather and temperature is suitable to prevention of spoilage of the meat or approximately 40-55 degrees on an average
cold feet	person becomes hesitant or afraid
come again when you can stay longer	next time you come to visit, please plan to visit longer
come git your vittles	come get your food

come hell or highwater
    This saying means that you are willing to do whatever it takes to overcome difficulty or obstacles.

The expression "come hell or high water" originated in America and was first in a printed reference from an Iowa newspaper, *The Burlington Weekly Hawk Eye*, dated May 1882: *"Since that time the best of my friends had become enemies and strangers have become friends. The devil had broken loose in many parts of the country and keeping up with the old saying, we've had unrevised hell and high water, and a mighty heap of high water, I tell you."*

(Google Dictionary, 2021)

come on in and sit a spell	come into my home and visit awhile
come on...shake a leg	start doing something faster
come out smellin' like a rose	end up doing very well
come to a screechin' halt	stop immediately
come to your senses	become logical and realize what is happening
comin' across too strong	being too forceful
comin' out of the wall	coming forth from no anticipated direction
comin' out party	revealing oneself
commence to	means to simply begin
company callin'	visitors appearing at one's house to visit with them
confound it	statement of complete frustration
consarn it	simple statement of frustration like "dadburnit", "confound it"
cooked done	well done or finished

cooked up a scheme	came up with or thought through a plan
cookin' on one burner	not thinking appropriately or thoroughly
cookin' up a storm	working or performing at the ultimate rate
cookin' up something	planning something
cookin' with gas now	working or performing at the very best rate
cool as a cucumber	very collected and calm
cool your heels	slow down or stop
coolin' his heels	slowing down or resting
corn-fed	raised on home cooking
cornbread and pot liquor	homemade cornbread and the juice from turnip greens cooked with bacon drippings for seasoning
cough up some money	reluctantly offered some money
coughin' my head off	coughing consistently
couldn't hit the broad side of a barn	terrible aim
countin' the days until...	waiting with great anticipation
country as turnip greens	turnip greens are a typical source of food for southern farmers
country as corn bread	authentic
courtin' disaster	taking a big risk
crack the window	open the window slightly
crack up	have an emotional breakdown
crammin' for a test	last-minute studying
cranky	cross and ill-natured
crazy as a betsy bug	quite emotionally disturbed
crazy as a loon	emotionally disturbed

cream of the crop	the best part of something.
creamed beef on toast	This is a military food served during the twentieth century. It can be made from chipped beef or hamburger. It is also called SOS or *"Shit on a Shingle"*. *(Naval Historical Foundation, 2021)*
credit good as gold	excellent credit
crick a small natural stream of water	
crick in my neck	a stiff or sore neck
crooked as a barrel of snakes	very vile
crooked as a snake	crooked
crusin' for a brusin'	putting oneself in a position of promoting a conflict
crybaby	immature
cry on my shoulder	lean on me
cryin' crocodile tears	false tears
cryin' shame,	a real shame
cryin' tears of joy	happy tears
cryin' your eyes out	very distraught
cryin' your head off	crying unconsolably
curiosity killed a cat...satisfaction brought him back	curiosity satisfied
cussin' up a storm	a real verbal abuse
cut a rug	excellent dancer
cut no slack	give no opportunity or second chance
cut out the foolishness	stop acting foolishly
cut out the noise	be quiet
cut the price	reduced for sale

cut you down to my size	bring you down to my level or lessen your advantage
cute as a bug	very cute
cute as a monkey	very cute
cute as a speckled pup	cute
cuttin' off your nose to spite your face	doing something that will not help but only hurt your purpose
cuttin' up	having fun by acting out

D [146]

dad blame it	saying of dismay to replace swearing
dad gum it	second saying of dismay alternate to swearing
dadburnit	yet a third saying of dismay alternate to swearing
damned if you do, damned if you don't	neither choice you make can be correct or work best for you
damn the mule...load the wagon	don't worry about anything but the task at hand, just proceed with the task
dark as a coal cellar	dark, cold, and very dark
darn-it	a saying of disgust without swearing
dead as a doornail	deceased or completely operable
dead as a mackerel	deceased or completely operable
dead ahead	straight ahead
deader than a doornail	old nails called doornails were square and the

51

	square head broke off used nails
dead cat on a line	a dead or closed issue
dead duck	deceased or completely operable
dead men tell no tales	dead men don't talk
dead-tired	extremely tired
deep water runs quietly	one who is reflective and deep thinking usually does so quietly
deaf as a post	can't hear at all or completely deaf
determined to self-destruct	participating in a behavior that is harmful to oneself again and again
devil-may-care attitude	an attitude of indifference
diamonds are for always	something that lasts forever and cannot be destructed
did ya et yet	have you eaten yet
digger-o-dell	grave digger, undertaker, or mortician
diggin' up dirt	researching and finding out inflammatory information about someone
dilly-dallyin'	wasting time not acting on something by procrastinating
dinner on the ground	a picnic served on the ground
dirty as a hog pen	extremely dirty
do tell	are you telling the truth
dodged the bullet	barely avoided a bad circumstance or reaction

don't borrow trouble	don't worry about something needlessly or before you have sufficient cause to worry
don't know if he's comin' or goin'	doesn't know what he is doing
do you ever scratch out	means speeding away at top speed in an automobile
do you feel run down	run down means tired, sick, or physically ill?
do you have a sweet tooth	do you like eating sweets
Doans Pills	medicine in the form of pills for aching backs
dodged the bullet	avoided what was coming his way
does that ever curl your hair	doesn't that really irritate you?
does your car have any pickup	does your car reach top speeds quickly?
doesn't have the sense God gave a goose	person is not very smart
doesn't have two dimes to rub together	person is extremely poor with no money
doesn't know which end is up	state of confusion
dog-tired	exhausted
doggone good	extremely good
doggone it	statement of irritation condemning an action
doin' something in a slipshod way	doing something poorly or in an ineffective and inappropriate manner
doin' the barn yard shuffle	trying to wipe farm animal excrement off your foot

doin' time in the pokie	spending time incarcerated, in jail or prison
dollar waiting on a dime	person of importance waiting on someone of lesser importance
done before you get started	defeated before you begin
don't be an old sore head	someone who is mad about almost everything
don't be so all-fired smart	don't act like you are an expert on something when you are not
don't be so crabbie	don't be irritable
don't beat around the bush	be direct in what you say
don't blow a gasket	don't get upset
don't count your eggs before they hatch	don't make plans prematurely before you are certain of the upcoming circumstances
don't get bent out of shape	don't get upset
don't get in a tizz	don't get upset
don't get me stirred up	don't upset me
don't give a hoot	don't have an opinion about something or care about the circumstances
don't give me any flax	don't cause me trouble or attempt to stop or interrupt me
don't give me that bull	don't give me ridiculous and false information
don't go flyin' off the hatch	don't be reactive before you think through something
don't go gettin' uptight about it	don't get frustrated, mad, or upset
don't have a dime to my name	completely out of money

don't have a leg to stand on	have no basis for a position or argument
don't have sense enough to get in out of the rain	person has no common sense and is a poor decision maker
don't have the time to fool around	do not want to be delayed with impertinent and information or actions that are not useful
don't have two pennies to rub together	very poor in terms of finances
don't hold me up	don't delay me
don't hold your breath	don't expect something to happen so don't hold your breath until it does
don't horse around	don't joke around
don't judge a man until you walk a mile in his shoes	don't be ready to condemn someone until you fully understand their circumstances
don't keep all your eggs in one basket	don't plan everything on one event or plan without alternative options
don't kid me	don't fool me or joke with me
don't know any more than the man in the moon	person knows nothing about what they are pretending to
don't know diddlie squat	don't know anything about what they are talking about
don't know "Gee from Haw"	This means that a person doesn't know the first thing about something. The

terms gee and haw are voice commands for an animal such as a mule to turn right or left, respectively.

don't know him from Adam's house cat completely unfamiliar with someone

don't know the truth from a hole in the ground you obviously do not know

don't know which end is up doesn't know what's happening

don't know which side your bread is buttered on don't know who or what to rely on for your benefit

don't let the door hit you on the way out please leave

don't let your guard down be aware

don't look a gift horse in the mouth don't question a fortunate occurrence

don't make a mountain out of a mole hill don't exaggerate

don't monkey around don't act ridiculous or foolish

don't put words in my mouth don't say that I have said something or tell me what to say

don't put off 'til tomorrow what you can do today do not procrastinate

don't rock the boat don't cause problems

don't screw up the works don't cause problems or interrupt with something

don't sell yourself short realize your potential and don't think of yourself as incapable

don't shoot 'til you see the white of their eyes take good aim

don't shout on the rooftop yet	don't be too quick to give out information to everyone
don't spill the beans	don't break a secret or tell something that is a confidence
don't squeal on me	don't be a whistleblower
don't start a free-for-all	don't start a fight
don't start something you can't finish	being slow to engage in conflict
don't string along	don't slowly hamper an action intentionally
don't take no wooden nickels	don't let anyone deceive you
don't take it lyin' down	don't accept something without resisting
don't talk back	don't be disrespectful in your verbal reaction to someone, especially someone older than you
don't tell me your troubles	don't complain to me
don't throw the baby out with the wash water	don't give up on an idea totally without examining its positive elements or points
don't tip your hand	don't let someone know what you are thinking and don't give them an advantage of finding out something until you are ready for them to do so as in playing a game of cards and holding your hand so that it can't be seen

don't try to butter me up	don't try to garner my favor for later advantage
don't wait 'til the eleventh hour	don't wait until the last minute as in the last clock hour of the day
don't want to hear any fish tales	tell me the truth
done his homework	knows what he is talking about
double or nothin'	a bet twice as much out of confidence
down and out	in a bad position much as a "boxer" who has lost the fight
down but not out	having problems but not defeated yet
down in the mouth	sad and forlorn or physically not feeling well
down in your back	your back is hurting you
down on your luck	you are having a bid time situationally or financially
down the drain	gone and completely unavailable and great loss
down the hatch	to swallow something
down to my last cent	financially at a great loss or very poor
draft dodger	someone who tries to avoid the military draft to serve their country in the armed services
drag up a chair and have a seat	sit down and converse
draggin' behind	coming up slowly or behind
drawin' to an end	coming to a finish
dressed fit to kill	dressed richly and well

dressed for Sunday go to meeting	wearing one's best clothes that are appropriate for church attendance
drinkin' mountain dew	drinking moonshine liquor
drippin' wet	as wet as if just leaving contact with water
drive a nail in my coffin	give an additional reason to condemn me
drivin' like a bat out of Hades	bats are the fastest fliers in the animal kingdom and one coming from "Hades" would ultimately be in a special hurry
drivin' me crazy	worrying someone considerably
drivin' me to distraction	worrisome
drivin' me up the wall	worrying someone considerably
droopy drawers	wearing your pants below your waistline so that they are saggy
drop a hint	give a hint
drop dead	fall to the ground dead
drop out of the picture	disappear from the situation
dropped the hammer on him	confronted and condemned him in a punitive manner
drunk as a skunk	very intoxicated
dull as a froe	a blunt sledgehammer device with a wedge on one end used for splitting shingles and cedar strips for birch bark canoes
dumb as a box of rocks	cognitively limited
dumb as a doornail	cognitively limited

dumb as an ox	cognitively limited
dumb Dora	cognitively limited
dumber than a stump	cognitively limited
dyin' off like flies	large numbers dying
dyed in the wool	totally convinced or totally convicted to something

E [28]

early bird catches the worm	ambition and proactive action gives an individual a definite advantage
early to bed and early to rise makes a man healthy, wealthy, and wise	one should get adequate rest and sleep to be healthy and productive
ears like an elephant	large-eared
easy does it	be careful
eat like a Turk	voracious appetite
eat up with	consumed with something
eating high on the hog	eating expensive food rather than plain food
eats like he has a hollow leg	voracious appetite
edgin' for time	avoiding or postponing something to gain some advantage
elbow grease	hard work effort
even a blind hog can stumble across acorn	**consequences** occur statistically in favor or against something happening
even a fish wouldn't get caught if he kept his mouth shut	don't share all you know with everyone to avoid negative consequences

every cow chews its own cud	everyone is responsible for their own actions and responsibilities
every dog has his day	every person eventually gets a turn in their favor
every house is not a home	a house is a building, a home is the emotional feeling and environment that is created by those living there
every tub must stand on its own bottom	everyone is responsible for their own actions
everybody must feather their own nest	everyone has to prepare for their needs and do what they can to put themselves in an advantageous position
everybody loves a lover	everyone enjoys a loving person and their actions
everybody's gossip is nobody's secret	if everyone knows something, it is not a secret to anyone
everyone must crawl before they can walk	there are steps in gaining skill or developing abilities
everything that glitters is not gold	things may look good initially and not be
eye ballin'	looking at something closely or examining it with scrutiny
eyes are bigger than your stomach	thought you were hungrier that you really were overestimating what you could eat or consume

eyes as big as saucers	facial expression with eyes extremely wide open
eyes like a hawk	very observant
eyes like pools of water	eyes that are watering or tearing up
eyes look like two fried eggs in a slop barrel	**their** eyes are red
eyes standing out on stems	wide-eyed

F [92]

face like a warthog ugly	
fading out of the picture	disappearing or becoming completely uninvolved in a situation
fair to middlin'	average
fair-weather friend	friendly only when it is advantages or good for someone and things are going well
fall from grace	lost support and approval
fallin' head over heels	becoming completely emerged in something, used in describing involvement in a personal romantic relationship
fallin' off to nothin'	losing weight, losing a great amount of weight
fannin' around	not wearing adequate clothing during cold weather as in going in and out of doors
far-flung	hard to believe
fast as a dose of salts through a widow woman	quickly
fast as greased lightnin'	very fast
faster than a jackrabbit	very fast

fat as a bucket of lard	very obese
fat as a hog	very obese
fat in the fire	aggravating or acerbating a situation by someone's action
fatback and sowbelly	country smoked bacon
fattie	derogatory name for an obese person
featherin' his nest	creating an advantageous situation for oneself through actions
feel like I've been run down by a truck	feeling physically or emotionally bad
feelin' his oats	feeling invincible
feelin' no pain	feeling invincible
feelin' poorly	physically ill or emotionally disturbed
feisty britches	a prissy person
fell flat on his face	completely failed
fell off a turnip truck	a complete novice with no experience
fell out	passed into unconsciousness
fess up	to confess or admit to something
few bricks short of a load	cognitively limited or mentally challenged
fight at the drop of a hat	difficulty with emotional control and prone to violence
fight to the finish	continue to work to achieve something until one of the parties is defeated
fightin' a lost cause	trying to accomplish something with little or no

	possibility of achieving your desired outcome
fightin' like dogs and cats	a severe fight
figure out something	reason and understand something
fillin' station,	a store and automobile garage for "filling" your car with gasoline or having your car serviced by an attendant
filthy as a pig sty	very dirty
filthy rich	very rich
finally came around	finally convinced
finders' keepers' losers' weepers	one's loss is another's gain
fine as frog hair	not fine at all as frogs do not have hair
finger-lickin' good, tasty	enough that one would like to lick their fingers used to taste the food
fire up a stove	start the stove usually as in building up a wood fire to cook over
first light	daylight
fishin' for a compliment	hinting or behaving in a manner to elicit a compliment
fit as a fiddle	in excellent physically or emotional health and condition
fit to be tied	a person is so upset that they might need to be restrained
fit to kill	describing the excellent and outstanding outfit and dress of an individual as in the scenario that they are

	dressed well enough for their own funeral
fixin' to go	getting ready to do something
fixin' to haul off and do it	getting ready to hastily begin something
fizzled out	gradually tired and exhausted to the point of nonexistence
flabbergasted	very surprised and shocked by something
flappin' in the breeze	used to describe someone talking incessantly and without discretion as "their lips flappin' in the breeze"
flat as a fritter	a fritter is a completely flat corn meal cake that is cooked in cooking oil in a skillet
flat as a pancake	very flat
flathead engine	A flathead engine, otherwise side valve engine, is an internal combustion engine with its poppet valves contained within the engine block, instead of in the cylinder head, as in an overhead valve engine
flew the coop	to escape or run away
flittin' around like a butterfly	in a social gathering going rapidly from one person to another like "a social butterfly"
floatin' on a cloud	going along smoothly
flop-eared	big extending ears

fly by night	operating in a manner to show no forethought or planning as in traveling in the dark at night
fly high as an eagle	to soar
fly in the buttermilk	a problem has arisen in a situation that is negative to the hopeful outcome or progress
fly in the ointment	a problem has arisen in a situation that is negative to the hopeful outcome or progress
fly in the sugar bowl	My Aunt Arlie announced that there was a "fly in the sugar bowl" when she had dessert following a meal
fly off the handle	become irrational and vocal, demonstrating uncontrollable behavior
fly with the crows...get shot with the crows	you are known for your associates and will be judged with them
flyin' down the road	driving very fast in a vehicle traveling in excess of the posted speed limit
flyin' high	doing very well
foamin' at the mouth	talking and very mad
following in his footsteps	copying someone
food is sky high	costs a lot of money
foolin' around	tampering with something that is not your business, or a second meaning is sexual behavior
forever and a day	always

footloose and fancy-free	unencumbered and free to act and behave
for a song	for very little money as a song sung by an individual in everyday life "costs" nothing
for Pete's sake	saying used to express frustration and annoyance
foreigner	someone not from a particular area who is not known by local individuals
forever more	always
forked tongue	deceitful
found his lucky star	has been very fortunate due to no earned reward but fortunate by chance
free, white and twenty-one	free to do whatever one wants without restriction
freezin' to death	very cold
fresh as a daisy	very clean and freshly adorned
from here to yonder	from the beginning to the end
frozen in his tracks	stopped abruptly as in the instinctive protective ability for an animal such as a rabbit or deer to stand perfectly still to avoid detection
front porch storytellin'	sitting on the front porch and sharing stories
full of vinegar	vinegar is acidic meaning that a person has spunk or pluck
full of yourself	really acting out

funny as a barrel full of monkeys	fun to associate with like an active playful group of monkeys
fuzzy	a man needing a shave

G [97]

get a grip	get in control of your emotions or actions
get ahead of yourself	act overconfident or plan prematurely
get out of hand	accelerate out of control
get the green light	get the go-ahead for something
get the hang of it	develop confidence or skill in doing something
gettin' along	socially interacting in a positive or productive manner
gettin' a lot of feedback	having conversation returned in a desirable and productive manner
gettin' hitched Sunday	getting married on Sunday
gettin' in shape	getting in good physical condition
gettin' money from him is like pullin' eye teeth	hard to get a person to give money
gettin' set	preparing to do something
gettin' squared away	getting organized or ready in a prepared way
gettin' up at the crack of dawn	getting up at sunrise
gettin' your ears lowered	get a haircut, making your ears look lower in your hairline
giddy as a schoolgirl	acting immature and impulsive

git fiddle	a violin
give him enough rope and he'll hang himself	given enough time a person will act in a manner to condemn himself/herself without interference from others attempting to do so
give me a break	excuse me
give me a hand	help or assist me
give my eye tooth	I would give anything to attain something
give out	exhausted
give the benefit of the doubt	consider the information and be sure that someone is at fault or guilty as in a person is innocent until proven guilty
give up the ghost	die
give you down the road	treated you very badly
God-fearin'	having a reverent feeling toward God or being a devout person.
go fetch a bucket of water	get a bucket of water
go fly a kite	dismiss yourself for whatever activity and leave me alone
go home to your sewer	go to others like yourself who are substandard
go jump in the lake	dismiss yourself for whatever activity and leave me alone
go off the deep end	get into something over your head without giving proper thought

go sit on a tack	dismiss yourself for whatever activity and leave me alone
go soak your head	dismiss yourself for whatever activity and leave me alone
go up in smoke	something is destroyed
go to great lengths	go to extraordinary lengths or make efforts to do something to an extreme or excessive degree
God must have loved poor folks...he	made so many of them Abraham Lincoln's quote (English Language and Usage, 2021)
goin' at a snail's pace	very slowly
goin' down the road lickety split	speeding down a road or hypothetical path faster than prudent or legal. ("Lickety Split III" is also the name of my 33.5 Hunter Sailboat)
goin' for broke	gamble in a situation, putting all your trust or effort behind something
goin' off half-cocked	proceeding totally unprepared as a situation originating from half-cocked when the position of the hammer of a firearm is partially but not completely cocked
goin' thata way	going in that direction
goin' to bed with the chickens	going to bed at sundown because that is when chickens roost

goin' to hell in a handbag	going poorly in a completely disastrous manner
goin' to pin your ears back	going to give you a reprimand
goin' to turn you every way but loose	going to administer physical punishment, as in administering corporal punishment to a child
gone batty	lost his/her reasoning ability or ability to make judgments, also called insane or crazy
gone busted	financially broken or without monetary funds
gone to the dogs	person has digressed to a very low ethical and moral stature
gone with the wind	simply gone without a trace
gonna get hitched	going to get married coming from the "hitching" of work animals to collectively pull a cart or wagon
gonna' meet your Waterloo	going to meet your ultimate failure or demise, coming from the Battle of Waterloo in which Napoleon met his final defeat
good as gold	as good or high standard that exists because gold is the most precious element

good for what ails you	good for any physical or emotional condition you may have
goosed me	to poke someone in the ribs
got a case of the blues	emotionally depressed
got a frog in my throat	hoarse throat sounding like the call of a frog
got a hankerin'	got an interest in or a strong desire to do something
got a head full of sense	very intelligent
got a head like a hammer	is hardheaded
got a loose screw	is not reasoning or thinking clearly
got a loose wire	is not reasoning or thinking clearly
got a lot of flak	received a bad reaction or condemning feedback
got a notion	inclined to do something
got ants in your pants	eager or anxious
got cold feet	reluctant or fearful
got him told off	dressed someone down, telling them exactly what you think about them or their negative behavior
got his head on straight	is clear thinking and very logical
got more money than Carter has pills	They contain bisacodyl that is used to treat constipation. (The Free Dictionary, 2021)
got on your soap box	taking a controversial verbal issue with something as speakers would do in the past,

standing on a stage or box to deliver an oration to the listeners

got the cart before the horse — acting in a premature fashion

got the fidgety jibbets — nervous

got the silly jiggles — in a jocular mood and laughing uncontrollably

got this job wrapped up — have a situation or task well on its way to be finished

got up before the chickens — awakened earlier than sunrise

got up on the wrong side of the bed — got up from bed in a bad mood

got what you deserve — what has happened to you is warranted and what one would expect because of your actions

got you pegged — got you figured out

got your goat — I have embarrassed you

gran young'un — grandchild

grandmaw was slow but she's old — you have no reason to be so slow

grasping at straws — trying to find any excuse or justification to attempt to maintain your position

graveyard shift — 12:00AM to 8:00AM

grease monkey — a mechanic

greasy spoon — an unclean restaurant, usually a small café

"Great Scott" — **This is** interjection of surprise or amazement. It most likely emerged as a phrase relating to Winfield Scott who was an American army general. He was 6'5" and weighed around 300 lbs. (Mental Floss, 2021)

green as a gourd	very much a novice with no experience as in a green gourd that is not mature
green as grass	very much a novice with no experience
grief-stricken	very much in grief
grinnin' from ear to ear	smiling broadly
grinnin' like a 'possum	smiling broadly
grinnin' like a Cheshire cat	smiling like the cat in "Alice and Wonderland"
grinnin' like a jenny eatin' saw briars	smiling or laughing with your mouth wide open
growin' like a weed	growing rapidly as in out of control
grits ain't groceries	grits are not adequate groceries implying that something is not adequate
guilty as sin	guilty without question
gun-shy	afraid because of previous experiences as an animal would be wary of a gun

H [207]

had a blowout	automobile car tire developed a puncture while in motion
had a close shave	came very close to something
had no business sticking your nose in it	something was not your business

74

have nothin' in common with you	I can't relate to you and have no common interests with you
hair like a Brillo pad	fuzzy or bushy headed with coarse hair
hair like a nickel mop	fuzzy or bushy headed with coarse hair
hair like grass won't grow on a busy street	a man's head is bald because he is thinking all the time
hair standin' on end	fuzzy, or bushy headed with coarse hair
half-baked	not rational
hammin' it up	pretending or enhancing something to gain prestige
hand me that thing-a-ma-jig	something you don't knows the name for
handwritin' on the wall	something that is very clear to you as if it were written on the wall in front of you for you to read
handy-andy	a person that can be extremely helpful especially in working
hang around	associate with
hang in there	don't quit
hangin' by a thread	barely maintaining a position comparison is to a loose button on a garment "hangin' by a thread" and about to be lost
hangin' onto his mother's coat tail	depending on his mother for support
hangout	a place to stay or spend time

happier than a lark	very lighthearted and happy
happy as a fox in a hen house	very happy and at a great advantage
happy as a June bug	very lighthearted and happy
hard as a rock	usually referring to someone being very stubborn
hard as nails	a very strong and immovable person
hard-hearted	a person without compassion
hard-luck story	an explanation for actions that is based on false excuses
has a forked tongue	a person who lies at times
has a hard row to hoe	a person has something to do that is very difficult and demanding?
has a sad awakenin' coming	person has a dismaying realization
has all his ducks in a row	has everything set up or is positioned in a way to accomplish something
has bad blood in him	is related to or comes from a bad family
has his head in the clouds	he is daydreaming or being
has his mind in the cellar	thinking obscene thoughts
has the big head	thinking too much of himself or arrogant?
have a ball	have a lot of fun
have a field day	have a great time

have a voice	to have an active role in deciding
have the gall	have the courage
haven't got enough room to change your mind	a very small space
haven't got the sense God gave a goose	very limited in terms of common sense, cognitive knowledge, or making decisions
haven't got the sense of a gnat	very limited in terms of common sense, cognitive knowledge, or making decisions
havin' a Come-to-Jesus meeting	telling someone exactly what you think about their behavior and setting them straight
Haven't hit a lick at a snake	haven't done any work at all
he always gets the hind tit	he always gets a bad deal as in suckling animals that don't get adequate access to feed
he broke her heart	hurt her deeply emotionally
he bucked the line	he got out of his placement and moved in front of another
he can weld everything but a broken heart	he is a master welder in working with metals
he carried it a little far	he went beyond reasonable bounds
he couldn't draw flies	can't draw
he did an about face	he completely changed his mind or his opinion

he dribbled out a little at a time	used it sparingly
he fell off the wagon	he resumed an undesirable behavior that he had previously stopped such as overeating or drinking liquor
he flipped his lid	he went crazy or became emotionally unglued
he had his bell rung	got hit with the ball...baseball or boxing match
he has a champagne appetite on a beer budget	he likes nice and expensive lifestyle or possessions but cannot financially afford them
he has a yellow streak down his back	he is a coward
he has me in a bind	a person is in a difficult position
he has such a line you could hang cloths on it	he is telling an obvious lie
he has too short a fuse	he gets upset too quickly
he is as dumb as a doorbell	he is mentally limited
he is lyin' like a rug	he is being untruthful
he is lyin' through his teeth	lying as he is talking to you
he jumped the gun	he acted too quickly as in starting a race before the firing of the starting gun
he kicked the bucket	he died
he knows I'm good for it	he knows I have the money and trustworthy reputation to pay him
he lives in a hole in the wall	he has a very small house
he lost his grip	he has faltered
he lost his rabbit foot on that	he was unlucky
he missed the boat on that one	he was wrong on that issue

he raked them over the coals	he berated them severely
he rooted me out of my job	he acted to cause me to lose my job in an unethical manner, politically called "backstabbing"
he seems crazy over her	he is obsessed with her
he should be horse-whipped	he should be physically disciplined
he sounds like a broken record	repeats himself
he split his britches on that one	he was wrong on something
he squirmed around like he had ants in his pants	he is very active
he stumbled upon it	he found out accidentally
he sure has a lot of brass on his face	he is very self-assured or bold. **he was all choked up** very emotional
he was caught with his hand in the cookie jar	he was caught "red-handed" in the act of doing something with evidence that is conclusive
he was caught with pie on his face	he was caught "red-handed" in the act of doing something with evidence that is conclusive
he who lies down with dogs rises up with fleas	you are affected by the company you keep
he who steals my purse steals trash	I have nothing worth taking
he would argue with a fence post	he is a very argumentative person
he would turn over in his grave	something that would be so disturbing or alarming

	to him that would cause him to rally from the dead
he'd tear up an iron ball	he is rough and destructive
he'll never get out of this world alive	everyone dies
he's a gem dandy	he is a great person
he's a quack	he's a poor doctor
he's a rich bug	he is wealthy
he's a stuffed shirt	he is aloof, boring, and arrogant, not relating to others at all because he thinks he is superior to all others
he's all ears	he is listening closely
he's an accident lookin' for a place to happen	he is on the track to fail
he's as straight as a row of corn	corn is planted in straight rows and this saying describes someone who is very straightforward, honest, and trustworthy
he's come to his jumpin' off place	he can take no more and endure no longer
he's comin' out on top	he is performing or winning ahead of his competitors
he's eatin' lunch with the worms	dead and buried
he's goin' straight	he is on the correct and right track
he's got a tiger by the tail	he is in a dangerous situation and is potentially destined to danger
he's got his head in the clouds	he is dreaming
he's got his nerve	he is unreasonably sure of himself

he's got that hangdog look	he has a sad and depressed facial expression
he's hung himself now	he has assured he will fail because of his actions
he's in hot water	he is in trouble
he's just draggin' around	he is just acting slowly
he's just holdin' on	he is just barely able to manage his behavior or actions
he's kind of slap-happy	he is happy in a silly way
he's like a pack rat	a collector
he's lit up like the fourth of July	he is very intoxicated
he's lost a screw	he is not thinking clearly
he's not worth his salt	he is worthless and not even worth the quantity of salt in his own body
he's not worth the powder to blow him up	he is totally worthless
he's pie-eyed	his facial expression is with eyes round and wide opened like the shape of a pie
he's plastered	he is drunk
he's so hen-pecked he eats scratch food	his wife totally controls him
he's taken a turn for the good	he is changing his behavior or physical state in a positive manner
he's taken a turn for the worst	his behavior or physical state is declining
he's the black sheep of his family	he is the different, odd, and less valued member of his family or group
he's twistin' my arm	trying to exert force on someone
he's worth about two cents with a	

hole in it	worth basically nothing
head and shoulders ahead	he is taking the lead or is winning with a very good margin
head like a ram and bound to butt	hardheaded and destined to cause conflict
head out this way	go this way
head over heels in debt	in debt so deeply that he may never be able to survive repayment
headstrong	obstinate
head-turnin'	good looking or attractive
headed in the right direction	proceeding in an appropriate and rational manner
heaping coals of fire on your head	getting yourself deeper into trouble
heart of gold	very good and loving person
heavin' at a gnat and swallowin' a camel	focusing on something small when there are greater issues at hand
heavin' like I'm wind-broke	out of breath or winded
heel and toe	Heel-and-toe shifting is an advanced driving technique used mostly in performance driving with a manual gearbox. (Track Days, 2021)
hell-bent	absolutely determined
hell's bells	exclamation of disbelief
help me tote in some wood	to help me carry some wood as tote means to

	carry, wield, or convey something
helpful as a hernia	anything but helpful
"Hemmin' and Hawin'" around	hesitating in speech

to discuss, deliberate, or contemplate rather than taking action

here today...gone tomorrow	not reliable
hi falootin'	behaving as if you are a very important person or behaving arrogantly
hide and watch	be quiet and just observe
hide your eyes	don't look or focus on something
high and mighty	arrogant and self-conceited
high as a kite intoxicated	
high falutin'	arrogant and falsely opinionated of himself
high muckety-muck	high social class
high water pants	pants that are too short and look as though they could withstand wading through high water without getting wet
higher than a kite	intoxicated
hind part before	backwards
his bark's worse than his bite	he seems rougher or more ill-tempered than he is
his word is as good as gold	he is totally trustworthy
hit a wall	come to an obstacle that halts your activity or progress
hit rock bottom	at your lowest point emotionally or financially
hit the deck	wake up and get out of bed

hit the ground runnin'	start immediately and quickly
hit the hay	went to bed
hit the trail	started on a trip
hit you so hard there won't be anything left but a greasy spot	hit and destroyed
hitch your wagon to a star	count on something that would make you ultimately successful
hittin' on all eight cylinders	performing well
hobblin' around like a mule with a broken leg	walking poorly
hog-wild	totally wild
hoity-toity	arrogant and thinking more of oneself than warranted
hold your horses	be patient
hold your voice down	be quieter
holdin' together with a wing and a prayer	barely holding together
holdin' your ground	standing firm
holding a pat hand	in card game you don't need any more cards in a business deal, you have a sure deal in progress without further assistance
hole in the wall café	small cafe
holler	to shout loudly
hollow	a low land area between hills or mountains usually associated with a creek or stream
home is where the heart is	home is the love and situation you have for family and friends

	regardless of a physical house or building
homemaker	a housewife who manages a home and is the hub of the family
honey-do list	the wife of the house has a list of chores "Honey would you please..."
honey catches more flies than vinegar	you will fare better if you are nice to people
hooptie do	"what is all the hooptie do" means what is all the fuss about. The term means an old and worn-out or junky car
hop a ride	take a ride with someone
hope your face doesn't freeze that way	you are making an ugly face
hoppin' mad	very angry
horny as a horn toad	sexually frustrated
horse hockey	horse manure!
horse play	rough play indoors
horse sense	common sense
hose pipe	outdoor faucet with a garden hose
hostess with the mostest	great hostess
hot as a cat on a hot tin roof	very hot and a cat on a tin roof burns its feet
hot as a depot stove	a depot stove is in a train station and is wood burning
hot as a firecracker	as hot as it gets
hot as a fox	very hot
hot as a lizard on a hot rock	very hot
hot as a pistol shot	burning hot
hot as a tater	very hot

hot as blue blazes	blue flames are the hottest flames in a fire
hot as can be	as hot as possible
hot as pepper	very hot
hot as the Fourth of July	very hot...usually about 95 degrees
hot shot	person who thinks he is special
hot to trot	woman looking for a man
hotter than grease in a skillet	burning hot
house duster	a dress-like smock worn by a woman to clean house or worn daily inside the house and not outside the house
house warmin'	an event to welcome someone to a new home
how are you doin'...fair to middlin'	are you ok...doing fair or average
humpday	Wednesday because it is in the middle of the week
hungry as a bear	ravenously hungry
hunted like a dog	tracked down
hurt his feelin's	made him sad
hush puppies	cornbread, onions, salt, pepper, and milk rolled into golf-sized balls and fried to be eaten with catfish, white beans, and French fries with a little tartar sauce and cocktail sauce
hustle and bustle	a lot of activity or work that is usually noisy

I [138]

I ain't the man I used to be
I cannot perform in the same way as previously

I cannot win for losing
I keep losing

I crashed
I failed

I'd give my eye teeth
I would give anything

I declare
exclamation of surprise

I didn't just fall off the turnip truck
I am not ignorant, inexperienced, or a novice

I didn't mean to get you all stirred up
I didn't mean to upset you

I died laughin'
I laughed until I got tired

I don't care one iota
I don't care the smallest amount. An iota is the smallest letter of the Greek alphabet.

I don't give a hoot
I don't care in the least

I don't give a rat's tail
I do not care in the least

I don't know...let me sleep on it
let me contemplate and reflect on it

I don't need someone to draw me a picture
I understand without further explanation

I don't think much of it
do not like something or look upon it favorably

If the shoe fits, wear it
if something describes your actions and fits your circumstances, accept the reprimand

I feel kind of let down
I feel disappointed

Ignoramus
a very ignorant person

I got laid off
got dismissed or terminated in employment

I got the wind of it
I became aware of it

I gotta fix my face
put on makeup

I guess you haven't been slapped down today
you are overly confident

87

I had a close call	I came close to experiencing something
I have a bone to pick with you	I have something to discuss with you as in a complaint or problem that I have with you
I have no idea	I am really at a loss for understanding
I haven't seen you in a month of Sundays	haven't seen you for a very long time
I hope you've learned your lesson	I hope you have gained understanding from this experience
I just can't get over it	I can't believe it
I just can't pin him down	I can't get him to commit
I know this like the back of my hand	I am very familiar with
I love you better than snuff and you are not even dusty	love you more than anything
I love you more than life itself	you very much
I need it like I would a bad cold	don't need it at all
In good repair	in good working shape
I swannee	exclamation of surprise and is a southern phrase for "I swear"
It was a frog croaker	so much rain it potentially drowned frogs
I think we're on the right track	we are taking the proper action or progressing in a prudent manner
I want a little peace and quiet	I need quiet time and a non-stimulating environment
I want you to put on your company manners	use your best manners

I wasn't born yesterday	I am aware of more than you give me credit for
I won't kowtow for anyone	I won't bow to anyone. From the Chinese meaning to bow or pay respect. (Google Dictionary, 2021)
I'd walk a mile for a Camel	I would really like a Camel cigarette
I'll be a monkey's uncle	term used to express complete surprise, amazement, or disbelief
I'll break you down like a shotgun	I will win in a physical or verbal altercation, with you breaking you down compared to the breakdown of a shotgun weapon prior to loading it with a shell
I'll carry you home	I will transport you home
I'll clean your plow	to physically or intellectually threaten someone
I'll knock a knot on your head	to threaten to fight and leave a contusion of someone's head
I'll knock the daylights out of you	I will knock you unconscious
I'll knock you into the middle of next week	I will knock you unconscious
I'll mosey on down to the store	go slowly
I'll pick you up	I will come by your residence and give you a ride

I'll put your name in the pot	consider selecting from applicants or petitioners you
I'll run you up to town	I will locate you
I'll send you packin'	I will send you away quickly
I'll skin you alive	be very angry with someone or punish them severely
I'll stick around	I will stay
I'll straighten you out	I will correct and stop your actions or behavior and put you on a different path
I'll turn you wrong side out	be very angry with someone or punish them severely
I'll whittle you down to my size	be very angry with someone and willing to fight to reduce them physically or emotionally to be in a situation or condition to be dealt with
I'll worry about that tomorrow	I will delay thinking about that until tomorrow
I'm a mind to	I am considering
I'm all in	I am all for it
I'm all out of steam	I am worn out physically, emotionally, or mentally
I'm all tuckered out	I am worn out physically, emotionally, or mentally
I'm fed up	I have taken all that I can withstand
I'm fixin' to	I am ready to do whatever
I'm goin' to break a limb to you	as threat of corporal punishment

I'm goin' to tell you up front	I will be honest with you initially
I'm gonna' knock you windin'	be very angry with someone and willing to fight them
I'm nobody's fool	basically not a fool
I'm not talkin' to hear my head rattle	I'm talking to you and not to myself
I'm on the lookout	I am watching out for something
I'm pullin' up stakes	moving
I'm runnin' short this month	running low on funds
I'm so hungry, I could eat a horse	very hungry as horses have been eaten at times of famine
I'm so hungry, my stomach thinks my throat's been cut	I am very hungry, and my stomach is growling because it has no food, and if it could reason, it might assume no food could pass because the throat had been cut
I'm tired of the whole shebang	I am tired of the whole situation
I'm tryin' to take a cold	I think I am becoming sick with a common cold
in a nutshell	in a very brief form or summary
in hindsight	the ability to realize and understand something about an event after it has happened
in the bag	accomplished or completed successfully

in the catbird seat	in a superior or advantageous position
in the driver's seat	in charge and doing well or making easy progress
in the snap of a finger	instantly
in the pokie	in jail
inner tubes	automobile and vehicle tires used to require inner tubes. Tires are now tubeless. Inner tubes could be repaired with patches and glue.
It's as wide as it is long	considering all possibilities there are no variations
I've got a gut feelin' about this	I just feel a particular way without evidence to back the feeling up
I've got bigger fish to fry	I have more important things to do or worry about
I've got the goods on you	I have the evidence on you
I've half a mind to	I am almost convinced or persuaded to do whatever
I've just been itchin' to tell you	I have been very anxious
I've run dry	I've run out
if he hadn't popped up	If he hadn't abruptly emerged
if that's what you think, you have another think coming	you should reconsider
If the good Lord's willin' and the creek don't rise	if everything goes alright and the creek does not rise over the bridge
if the shoe fits wear it	If you are guilty accept the circumstance
if wishes were horses, beggars	

could ride	we don't always or even frequently get what we wish for
if you can't take the heat, get out of the kitchen	If you are not willing or capable of taking pressure or criticism, don't get involved
if you don't like it, you can lump it	I don't care if you like it, you can bear it anyway
if you know what's good for you	should consider the outcome of your actions
if you plan on fightin' me, you'd better bring your lunch	it will be a long, long fight
if you're waitin' for me, you're backin' up	I am ready
if you're waitin' for me, you're draggin' your feet	I am ready, but are you?
ill as a hornet	very mad
I'm fixin' to try my hand	starting to try to do something or perform an activity
in a bind	in an uncomfortable position
in a family way	pregnant
in a pig's eye	never and under no circumstances

(Collins, 2021)

in debt over my head	in debt for way more than can possibly be repaid
in earshot	within hearing range
in one ear and out the other	not listening to what I say
in the mood	in a romantic mood
in the same boat	be in the same unfortunate circumstances as others

Indian Giver

Indian giver is an American expression used to describe a person who gives a "gift" and later wants it back. This saying comes originates from a cultural misunderstanding between European settlers and Indigenous people.

Europeans saw what was given as a gift, The Indigenous people looked at the situation as a trade of equal value. (Urban Dictionary, 2021)

it ain't over 'til the fat lady sings

This is a colloquialism which means one should not presume the outcome of a situation that is still in progress

it fizzled out

the situation or event dissipated

it is an eyesore

something that is substandard and unsightly

it makes my flesh crawl
it is very repulsive to me

it makes my toenails curl
it is upsetting

it makes time fly
keeps one occupied

it takes one to know one
you are criticizing someone who is just like you

it turns my stomach
it upsets me

it'll all come out in the wash
all will eventually be disclosed or discovered

it's a cat fight
two women fighting

94

it's a piece of cake	it is easy
it's a quarter waiting on a dime	the person waiting is more important
it's all downhill from here	things will only get worse
it's as broad as it's long	two things are equal
it's close enough for government work	the phrase was created in World War II with the usage meaning that a product met the highest standards of quality and would not be accepted by the Uncle Sam if it did not meet those standards. As early as the 1960s it became used in a disparaging manner.

(Wiktionary, 2021)

it's come up a cloud	clouds have formed in the sky overhead
it's good for what ails you	it is good for your physical health
it's in the genes	you are genetically destined
it's no big deal	it's not a big issue or problem
it's no skin off my nose	it's presents no problem to me
it's the squeaky wheel that gets the grease	the most noticeable (or loudest) problems are the ones most likely to get attention
it's water over the dam	it's something that has already occurred and

it's your dime...start talkin'

should be passed over if not forgotten

you initiated this, so you begin talking.

This comes from the era (US) when there was payphones and those phones charged ten cents a call. "It's your dime, start talking" was a brusque greeting indicating that you're the one who paid for the call so don't waste your time.

(Urban Dictionary, 2021)

J [24]

jabberin' like a magpie   talking incessantly

jabberwock   a person who walks incessantly

jack of all trades   a person who can do many types of work but is not a master at any of them

jailbird   a person in jail or prison

jalopy   old motor vehicle in bad state of repair

Slayden Children

Front Seat: Woodroe Slayden at wheel and Mabel Slayden Hodge beside him

Back Seat: Odessa Slayden Norfleet (left) Edna Slayden Bell (right)

Story from Then... *"Jalopy"* Charles Alvin Slayden

During the Great Depression (mainly the 1930s), everything was scarce including work. Grandfather Slayden was a carpenter and there was no work to be found in Clarksville. He took his family to Central Florida, where work was rumored to be more prevalent and where we had several relatives. He made a wooden box about six feet by four feet and fastened that on the rear bumper of the car of his old 1920s car. When they started out on the trip, he loaded that wooden box with jellies and preserves that my grandmother had made. Travelers included my grandfather, his two sons, and my great aunt and uncle. My grandmother and their youngest son had already ridden the bus a couple of weeks earlier to Mount Dora. My grandfather had several loaves of bread as well as the jelly and peanut butter. Peanut butter and jelly sandwiches were what they had to eat all along the way. You must realize that at this time there were no interstate highways and even if they had been in the situation where they had money for anything but gasoline, there were no restaurants or quick shops. The trip took them through Georgia and every little town between Clarksville, Tennessee, and Mount Dora, Florida. The total travel time for the trip was four days. They slept on pallets beside the road at night. Every time they encountered a small boy rolling a tire down the road, they would stop and give him a quarter for the tire and tied it to the side of the car. At any given point, they had five or six tires tied to the sides of the car. During the trip they had some forty flat tires or blow outs. At that time automobile tires had tubes. This was a problem too and they had a patch kit with rubber patches and glue to repair the tubes. Even though my grandfather was a carpenter by trade, he had previously attended mechanic school and could work on cars. The older model cars had no computers or sophisticated electronics and were easier to work on.

On the second day of the trip, the transmission on his car went out. There was a gear problem. He pulled the car off the side of the road and jacked the car up with the car jack and some large rocks he found in a ditch on the side of the road. Here beside the road was where he tore the transmission down to see what was wrong with it. He sent his brother to town via a by passerby motorist to obtain the piece needed to repair the transmission. When his brother returned with the five-dollar part, he repaired and reinstalled the transmission right there on the side of the road. When he finished everyone got back in the car and when he put the car in first gear, it ran in reverse. When he put it in second gear, it ran in reverse. When he put the car in reverse, it ran in reverse. Everyone climbed out of the car and the men jacked the car up once again and began to tear the transmission down for the second time. My aunt decided that she would walk to a nearby farmhouse just up the road. When she got to the house, a woman met her at the door and invited her to come in. When she told of their predicament, the farmer's wife made sandwiches for them and made a jug of lemonade. She then asked what else that she might do to help. My aunt was a blatantly honest and direct person and she replied, "What I would really like is a bath because I am hot and tired, and we have been traveling for two days." The farmer's wife said that she certainly could have a bath. My aunt walked back down the road refreshed. After sharing the sandwiches with everyone they got in the car. This time the transmission problem was repaired. They continued their trip. During these hard times, people helped each other out. This is only one example of how my grandfather Charles Alvin Slayden was a hardworking

Katie bar the door

watch out and prepare for the worst

keep a stiff upper lip
remain composed

keep it to a low ebb
at a low point, in a state of decline, or depression

keep it under your hat
keep it secret

keep the home fires burnin'
remember someone and maintain their welcome

keep your cottin' pickin' hands to yourself

Cotton-picking is an intensifier used as a general term of disapproval. A substitute for the word "damned". The origin of the word came from the term "cotton-picking" in the southern states of the USA where it was usually pronounced cotton-pickin'. It began life in the late 1700s and differs from the 19th century Dixie term, "cottonpicker", in that the latter was derogatory and racist, whereas "cotton-picking" referred directly to the difficulty and harshness of gathering the crop. This didn't extend to the specific expression "keep your cotton-picking hands off of me". This no doubt alludes to the rough and calloused hands that picked cotton.

keep your nose to the grindstone	keep working
keepin' company	dating someone
keepin' the road hot	constantly on the move
key to my heart	you can open my heart to love
kickback	be at leisure or relax
kick'in up his heels	having fun without inhibition
killin' time	an activity that you do while trying to pass time and not be bored
kin folks'	people you are biologically related to or related to through marriage
kinda got carried away	overreacted
kinda left it hanging	unfinished
kinlin'	small pieces of wood used to start a fire or the act of starting a fire, causing a flame to begin burning
kiss my foot	a saying to insult someone if you are upset with them and want to dismiss them
kiss of death	an action or event that will cause certain failure
kiss your money goodbye get	ready to lose your money with no hope of getting it back
kissed the Blarney Stone	The Blarney Stone in Ireland supposedly gives good luck to those who kiss it

survivor. They reached Florida and found work. My grandfather loved family and was a God-fearing man. He was also a World War I veteran having served in France. He took care of his family and did everything in his power to provide for their needs. Hard work, persistence, intelligence, and ingenuity always guided his outcomes.

Johnny-come-lately	a newcomer or late starter in a particular activity
jug head	an alcoholic
jump-jig	a two-wheeled cart

Story from Then... *"Jump-Jig"* William Henderson Robbins

My great-great grandfather used a small two-wheeled cart pulled behind a horse to deliver the mail. William Bailey's house was in Faxon, Tennessee. It was a grocery store and post office. William Henderson Robbins would be gone two to three days at a time delivering the mail from Faxon to north of Big Sandy to Pace on Bennett's Creek. The mail was carried in a two-wheeled cart called a "jump-jig" pulled by horse or mule. William was known to say "Here we go Jack..." as he started his trips on his mail route.

William Henderson (Henry) Robbins was my great-great grandfather. He was a Civil War soldier in the Confederacy joining Wilson's Calvary May 16, 1863, and was a soldier to the end of the war. He served with Wilson Calvary Company of the Napier Division and has a Government Marker for the C.S.A. 21st TN Wilson's Calvary. He has a Government Marker Forrest Calvary C.S.A. After the Civil War he delivered the mail by horseback operating out of his father's country store and post office. He is buried in the Wynn Cemetery East of Faxon, Tennessee. William was the last surviving Confederate soldier in Benton County and last surviving soldier on either side of the great conflict. He was Benton County's oldest citizen and last survivor of the Civil War. He died at the age of ninety-five.

When I visited the Tennessee State Department Archives in Nashville, Tennessee, I found microfiche containing letters that William Robbins (my great-great-grandfather) wrote to the United States Government requesting a pension when he was around ninety years old. The author found support letters from officials in Benton County stating that the "old soldier" was about blind and deaf and that he told them that he didn't sign any papers at the end of the Civil War. He simply stated that "he got done and went home". He was a Confederate soldier all his life. He did receive a pension from that time on until his death in the amount of $86.00 a month.

WILLIAM HENRY ROBINS

Camden—Funeral services were held Monday at the family cemetery near Faxon, for William Henry Robins, Benton County's oldest citizen and last survivor of the Civil War. He was 95. Services were conducted by the Rev. H. E. Trevathan. Mr. Robins joined Wilson's Cavalry May 16, 1863, and served in the Confederate Army until the close of the war. He lived in Benton County all of his life.

He is survived by seven children, Mrs. J. C. Parker of Camden, G. W. Robins and Mrs. Della Allen of Big Sandy, F. W. Robins and Miss Tennie Robins of Chicago, Ill., J. C. Robins of Wayne, Ark., and Miss Mattie Robins of Clarksville, Tenn. He also leaves thirty-three grandchildren, and nineteen great-grantchildren. *June 1939*

Source: The Camden Chronicle, July 29, 1938

jump-start — to start an engine by temporary connection to an external power source

jump to conclusions — speedily arrive at a conclusion without adequate information

junkman	operator of a junkyard or recycling center for automobiles and vehicles
jury-rigged	as an adjective jury-rigged means a temporary makeshift arrangement or setup. Sailors would rig the jury after a storm if their sails were damaged. This was a temporary setup to get back to land.

(Dictionary.com, 2021)

just a spit in the ocean	just a small amount
just about fed up	just about saturated with something and resisting further discussion or action
just as sure as the day is long	absolutely assured
just can't get a foot hold	can't get a good start
just checked out	just quit
	Old Sailing Ships
just draggin' around	performing slowly or moving slowly
just for the heck of it	just for fun
just got creamed	defeated
just had a brainstorm	had a novel thought or inspiration
just keep your pants on	be patient
just stoppin' up your ears	not listening

K [30]

Kapoot	fed up tired or done with or broken

102

Katie bar the door	watch out and prepare for the worst
keep a stiff upper lip	remain composed
keep it to a low ebb	at a low point, in a state of decline, or depression
keep it under your hat	keep it secret
keep the home fires burnin'	remember someone and maintain their welcome

keep your cottin' pickin' hands to yourself

Cotton-picking is an intensifier used as a general term of disapproval. A substitute for the word "damned". The origin of the word came from the term "cotton-picking" in the southern states of the USA where it was usually pronounced cotton-pickin'. It began life in the late 1700s and differs from the 19th century Dixie term, "cottonpicker", in that the latter was derogatory and racist, whereas "cotton-picking" referred directly to the difficulty and harshness of gathering the crop. This didn't extend to the specific expression "keep your cotton-picking hands off of me". This no doubt alludes to the rough and calloused hands that picked cotton.

keep your nose to the grindstone	keep working
keepin' company	dating someone
keepin' the road hot	constantly on the move
key to my heart	you can open my heart to love
kickback	be at leisure or relax
kick'in up his heels	having fun without inhibition
killin' time	an activity that you do while trying to pass time and not be bored
kin folks'	people you are biologically related to or related to through marriage
kinda got carried away	overreacted
kinda left it hanging	unfinished
kinlin'	small pieces of wood used to start a fire or the act of starting a fire, causing a flame to begin burning
kiss my foot	a saying to insult someone if you are upset with them and want to dismiss them
kiss of death	an action or event that will cause certain failure
kiss your money goodbye get	ready to lose your money with no hope of getting it back
kissed the Blarney Stone	The Blarney Stone in Ireland supposedly gives good luck to those who kiss it

kissin' cousins,

A "kissing cousin" is any cousin that is not a first cousin. In most places in the world, first cousins may not have sex and have babies. But, in most cultures second cousins, and higher can have sex and babies. Degree of cousinship is determined by how many generations the shared ancestor is removed from the individual closest to the generation of the shared ancestor.

If we share the same grandparent, we are first cousins and therefore should avoid physical encounters with each other which might lead to sex.

Source: Urban Dictionary

knee-high to a grasshopper	a very small person
knee-deep	deeply or significantly involved
knock on wood	a superstition which is supposed to ward off or prevent bad luck or misfortune
knock the breath out of you	hit in the stomach causing one to be winded
knock your lights out	got hit hard
knuckle sandwich	a punch in the mouth

L [134]

labor of love — something done for no pay but for conviction

ladies of the evenin' — prostitutes

lady's man — a fancy and well-dressed man that attracts women

lamebrain — a stupid person

lame duck — someone who has little influence because of his/her limited power and position

Land o' Goshen! — an old-fashioned mild exclamation of surprise, alarm, dismay, annoyance, or exasperation

land so poor it wouldn't grow cockleburs — these plants are drought-resistant and very hardy spreading easily

large helpin' — a large serving

larger than life — very authentic

last gets the hash — hash is a dish made of leftover meat and vegetables after a previous meal of those items

last of a breed — last of a kind

last one in is a cow's tail — a derogative term for taunting the last person to do something

last one is a rotten egg — a derogative term for taunting the last person to do something

late as Moody's goose — someone who is very late

later than Snyder's goose — another late goose (see above)

laugh and the world laughs with

106

you...cry and you cry alone	people are much more willing to be happy than share sorrow
laugh it off	laugh and go on and don't dwell on something
laughed his head off	laughed hysterically
laughin' out of the other side of your mouth	the events will change against you and the humor may change
lay a fire	the act of stacking kindling (kinlin') breaking the wood in small pieces to expose it to more oxygen to make it burn faster
layin' down the law	firmly stating what is expected of someone to them verbally
layin' rubber	spinning the tires on asphalt
lead a horse to water but you can't make him drink	you can provide an opportunity to someone, but you cannot force them to take that opportunity
leapin' for joy	physically and verbally demonstrating happiness or joy
leaves falling like rain	leaves falling like raindrops
leavin' like rats abandoning a sinking ship	people leaving quickly in all directions
left at the altar	deserted at their wedding by one's partner cancelling

	the marriage at the last minute
left-handed doin' things	a criticism or insult disguised as a compliment
left-handed monkey wrench	A fictitious tool or joke because a monkey wrench has no left-handed or right-handed version
legs like a killdee	skinny legs as the small skinny "killdee bird" (slang for killdeer).
let a sleepin' dog lie	don't stir up a situation
let me hope you	let me help you
let me sleep on it	let me think about it
let off steam	relieve tension
let the cat die	"Let the Cat Die" – which means, stop pumping your legs while swinging and let the swing stop moving on its own.
let the wind out of his sails	caused him to lose confidence
let your hair down	relax
let's talk turkey	let's talk honestly
let's wrap up this little ball of yarn	finish
libel to	apt to do something or likely to do something
lickety split	quickly or a fast as possible
lickin' his wounds	feeling sorry for himself after a fight or defeat
life in the easy lane	life is easy and going smoothly
light as a feather	very light
light of the moon	seeing by the light of the moon

lightnin' never strikes twice in the same place	you won't experience that again
lights on and nobody's home	mentally deficient
like a bull in a china shop	clumsy and not graceful
like a fish outta water	out of your element or dealing with something you are not used to
like a slow boat to China	moving very slowly
like a snake in the grass	sneaky or hidden from view intentionally
like an anchor around your neck	a restriction or situation of being hampered
like Bon Ami...ain't scratched yet	Bon Ami, French for "good friend", is a brand of household cleaner products
like feeding fuel to a flame	increasing the acceleration of a situation in a negative manner
like herdin' cats	difficult to direct or lead a group of people
like fittin' a square peg in a round hole	trying to get something to work with great difficulty
like lookin' for a needle in a haystack	almost impossible to find
like pullin' eye teeth	doing something that is very difficult and painful or stressful
like the tail that wags the dog	a powerful or important person is controlled by someone or something less important or powerful
like to come a courtin'	would you like to date
like tryin' to drown a duck in water	very difficult to do
like tryin' to get used to a tack in your shoe	impossible to do

like white on rice	extremely close to something
I'll jerk a knot in your neck	means to physically threaten someone
limp as a dishrag	very limp
listen up	to get someone's attention and to admonish them to listen carefully
little bit of nothin'	absolutely nothing
little house out back	outdoor toilet or out house
little old mickey mouse job	a small and insignificant job
little upstart	an upstart is someone who's cocky and arrogant, and who doesn't show much respect for other people
livin' it up	living richly
livin' above his means	living a lifestyle that he cannot financially afford
livin' from hand to mouth	to have just enough money to live on and nothing extra
livin' high on the hog	living well as in eating more desirable portions of pork
livin' it up	living or acting extravagantly
livin' off the fat of the land	to live off the fat of the land means to live well, to live off the surrounding abundance
livin' on borrowed time	to continue living after a point at which you might easily have died

loaded for bear	prepared to accomplish the task as in having a gun loaded with the correct caliber to kill a bear
lockin' horns	to get into an argument as a comparison to two deer that lock horns while fighting
loner	an individual who prefers to be alone or socially isolated
long arm of the law	the law extends everywhere
long gone	gone for a long time ago
long green with a short future	paper money soon to be spent
long in the tooth	Someone or something that is old in age. This phrase is commonly used to refer to people or things that are along in years. All teeth wear down in time and this saying originally referred to animals.
long on words short on wisdom	talks quite a bit but has no good information or advice regardless of all the dialogue
long-winded preacher	a clerical or religious person who speaks for an extended period
look before you leap	consider the consequences before you act
look like you been through the mill	to have had a lot of problems or a very difficult time

look on the bright side	be positive
lookin' for a handout	seeking something for free
lookin' for a soft place to land	looking for a good position to acquire
lookin' for trouble	behaving in a manner that would elicit trouble
lookin' googled-eyed	eyes look red and irritated and very large
lookin' like the cat that swallowed the canary	looking guilty
lookin' peaked	having a sickly appearance
lookout man	a person to keep watch for some anticipated event
looks good enough to eat	looks delicious
looks like a drowned rat	looks very wet and soggy
looks like you just stepped out of a ban box	look nice in appearance with special clothes and dressed well
looks like she's been beat with an ugly stick	she is an ugly person
looks like warmed-over death	looks physically bad as in a dead person
looks like we're in for a blow	in for a storm
loose as a goose	has diarrhea
lop-eared mule	a mule with floppy ears
lop-sided	sagging or leaning to one side or the other
Lord have mercy	Compassion leads a person to have mercy, which is like forgiveness
losin' ground	to lose any advantage or acquired progress
lost all sense of time	unaware of the passage of time
lost and found	an area, box or office that receives articles that are

	turned in by individuals who found them in hope that the person who lost them will return and claim them
lost as a fish out of water	totally out of place and in an environment or condition that is completely uncomfortable or not accustomed to
lost as last year's Easter egg	totally lost
lost cause	something that cannot be accomplished
lost his bearin's	lost his directionality
lost his looks	has declined in physical attraction
lost his marbles	he is mentally ill, crazy, or insane, causing him to not think rationally
lost his nerve	he has become afraid to proceed
lost his prime	he has passed the time in his youth when he was physically, mentally, and emotionally superior to his age and present condition
lost his will to live	is depressed and possibly suicidal
lost in a fog	confused
lost in thought	concentrating in deep thought
lost my hankerin' to go	have a desire to go
lost my touch	lost my ability or skill
love 'em and leave 'em	love someone and leave them and then love

	another and leave them as well
love is a two-way street	two individuals are involved in a romantic relationship acting and thinking from two separate perspectives
love is blind	many times it is difficult to clearly and objectively evaluate someone that you love
lovesick	in love with a person so much that one feels physically ill
lovesick cow	a term comparing someone to a cow that is agitated because she is in season and between a recent calf and the next mating process
love that won't let you go	a love that you cannot forget or put aside
low and lonely	depressed and lonely
lower than a snake's belly	the lowest
luck of the draw	by chance
lyin' like a rug	a rug lies on the floor

M [63]

mad as a hornet	mad with vengeance
mad as a sore-tailed cat	extremely irritated
mad as an old wet hen	extremely irritated
made a monkey of him	made him look ridiculous
made a spectacle of herself	she behaved in a ridiculous manner
made him back down	made him retreat
made me see stars	struck me on the head

made your bed	created your own situation
make a point of	take the time and make the effort to do something
make hay while the sun shines	work or proceed while you have time as in the time that the sun is up when working in a pasture harvesting hay
makes him feel ten feet tall	makes him proud and confident
makin' advances	flirting with someone
makin' a lot of commotion	making noise and causing confusion
makin' eyes	meeting eyes with someone attempting to flirt in a sexual manner with them
makin' her an honest woman	marrying her and making the relationship legal
makin' music	playing an instrument or playing in a band
makin' out	sexual behavior such as hugging, kissing, and fondling
makin' out like a fox in a hen's house	doing very well and benefitting without much effort
makin' whoopie	making love
makin' mistakes by the numbers	making numerous mistakes
mama's little touch me not	a clingy child who runs to his/her mother to avoid conflict with other children
man of the cloth	a clergy

many hands make light work	a task is easier if you have numerous people working on it
markin' time	waiting
marriage is a two-way street	two individuals make a marriage
marriage is like a bumpy road	marriage has its difficult times and problems to overcome
mealy-mouthed someone is unwilling to speak in a manner that is clear and truthful	
mean as a junkyard dog	mean and aggressive
mean as a woman on wash day	wash day was a challenge for women when they used wash tubs and wash boards to clean clothes, usually putting them in less than a good mood
mean as sin	mean as can be
meek as a lamb	retiring and timid
meet yourself comin' again	turning around in circles
mess of fish	the collection of fish that you catch in one fishing episode
mess of greens	the quantity of turnip or collard greens that you pick at one time on one occasion to cook as a singular meal
messin' around	doing something in a haphazard manner
met his match	has found his equal
metal he's made of	what his temperament and convictions are

"Might as well...too wet to Plow"	do one thing because you can't do something else as in a farmer who can't plow because his field is too wet
Mighty oaks from little acorns grow	big things come from small beginnings
mind in the gutter	thinking obscene or vulgar thoughts
mind like a steel trap	forgets nothing
misery loves company	if a person is miserable, they like comfort or the interaction with someone who can relate to them or give them sympathy
missed your callin'	you got into the wrong vocation
mixed messages	a partly positive and partly negative reaction
money burnin' a hole in your pocket	anxious to spend your money
money to burn	more money than you need for your regular expenses
morals of an alley cat	no morals or ethical convictions especially applied to promiscuous women
more kids than she can shake a stick at	numerous children possibly too many for her to control
more money than he knows what to do with	considerable financial advantage

more than he bargained for	the consequences are worse or more astringent than he anticipated
more than one way to skin a cat	there is more than one way to do something
mortgaged to the hilt	someone with so much debt that he/she is unlikely to be able to repay it possibly leading to bankruptcy
mossin' on	going on one's way slowly
motor mouth	someone who talks too much or to excess
motor purring like a cat	motor of an automobile running very smoothly as it should like the purring of a cat
mule skinner	a person who drives a team of mules
must be out of his mind	must not be thinking clearly
must be out of his tree	must not be thinking clearly
must have a straight gut	can eat so much that his intestines must be straight allowing them to hold more food
my head hurts so bad I can't see what I'm saying	I can't concentrate
my hearts runnin' away	my heart is beating very fast
my old bucket of bolts	my old car
my old coon hunting dog	a dog used for hunting raccoons with a hunter
my right-hand man	my best helper and aid

my Sunday pants   slacks or pants that you wear as dress clothes

N [42]

naked as a jay bird   wearing nothing because birds don't wear clothes

necktie party   a hanging execution party or group of individuals who are poised to perform a hanging either literally or figuratively

neckin'   kissing

needle nose   sharp and pointed nose

needs for someone to build a fire under him   he requires the pressure of others to act

needs his pants torn up   he needs to be spanked or corporally punished

nervous as a bowl of jello   very nervous

nervous as a bride on her weddin' night   very nervous and apprehensive

nervous as a cat in a room full of rockin' chairs   very nervous and apprehensive

never darken my door again   don't ever bother me again

nice nasty   When a person speaks pleasant words in a sarcastic or condescending manner, and you realize that they were really insulting you after your conversation is over. My mother had a very different meaning for this idiom. She would say that someone was nice nasty meaning that they were obsessed by dirty things including cleaning incessantly.

(Urban Dictionary, 2021)

nincompoop

This is a silly-sounding word that's also kind of old-fashioned like the word ninny. This word means a foolish acting person.

ninnie goose

a silly-sounding word that's also kind of old-fashioned like the word ninny follow by the word goose that is a rather dumb bird

nit-pickin'

the phrase comes from the task of removing the tiny eggs of lice (nits) from someone's hair and clothing which is a tedious activity

nitty-gritty

basic

no fool like an old fool

old people can be foolish and sometimes act more so than young people

no holds barred

the literal meaning is with no restrictions. The origin of the word comes from it use in wrestling competitions.

no pain no gain	little is achieved without cost, hard work and effort or investment
no sweat	no problem
nose for news	good at finding things out
nosy	adjective for a person who is involved too much in other's business or personal affairs
not enough gumption to do it	lacks the initiative, aggressiveness, or resourcefulness to accomplish something

Source: Dictionary.com

not enough room to cuss a cat without gettin' fur in your mouth	a very small space
not enough sense to get in out of the rain	senseless
not in my wildest dreams	statement of surprise and amazement saying that one would never have imagined it
not in this world	never
not just whistlin' Dixie	not kidding
not out of the woods yet	this saying describes the health of an individual who is still in danger of physically getting worse or dying
not playin' with a full deck	not thinking with full mental ability
not the only fish in the lake	not the only person to associate with or seek out to date

not today	I'll not be fooled yet
not worth a nickel	worthless
not worth a plug nickel	totally worthless
not worth shootin'	worthless
not worth the powder to blow him up	worthless
not worth two cents with a hole in it	worthless
now the ball's in your court	now it's your turn
now the truth comes out	now the situation is understood fully
now you're cookin' with gas	doing very well
now you're percolatin'	A "percolator" is a pot used for brewing coffee quickly. Someone "percolatin'" is becoming lively.
now you're showin' your true colors	This saying means to show your real character or personality. It originates from ships showing the flags of their countries.
nuttier than a fruit cake	crazy or insane

O [47]

o'bother	exclamation of dismay
off color comment	insulting or inappropriate comment of a sexual nature
off handed	casual comment of negative nature offered in an insulting manner
off on a wild goose chase	on a fool's errand or pursuing an impossible goal
old as dirt	ancient as the beginning of time
old as Methuselah's father	Methuselah was a Biblical patriarch who is said to

have died at the age of 969 and the longest-lived figure in the Bible.

(Christianity, 2021)

old as the hills — ancient as the beginning of time

old enough to know better but too young to care — being foolish and using poor judgment

old geezer — old man who is contrary or difficult to deal with

old run over shoes — shoes that are worn by a person's feet to the extent that they are mis-shapened

older than dirt — old as the dirt that the Earth is composed of

on a path of self-destruction — is performing and acting in a manner that will lead to his destruction without interference from anyone else

on good terms — on good or friendly terms with someone

on his death bed — is dying

on my list — I have taken note of something and added it to the things I need to attend to

on the last leg of the journey — finishing the journey

on the other hand, — here is a contrasting opinion to what was just stated

on the right track — pursuing something with the correct approach

on the trail

once in a blue moon

solving a problem or mystery

This term means a very rare event. The term has traditionally, in the Maine Farmer's Almanac, referred to an "extra" full moon, where a year which normally has 12 full moons has 13 instead. This happens every two or three years. The phrase in modern usage has nothing to do with the actual color of the Moon, although a visually blue Moon (the Moon appearing with a bluish tinge) may occur under certain atmospheric conditions such as volcanic eruption or fire that release particles in the atmosphere of just the right size to preferentially scatter red light.

Source: Wikipedia

one board short of a load

not complete

one foot in the grave

very ill possibly facing death

one foot in the grave and the other on a banana peel

very ill possibly facing death

one for the road

one last drink or story before departure

124

one man's junk is another man's treasure	people see different value in things
one oar in the water	possibly only half prepared
one of a kind	unique and the only one in existence
one picture is worth 1,000 words	an illustration adds concreteness
one sandwich short of a picnic	not cognitively or mentally competent
'oopin' up	raising up from a chair or a sitting position
opening a can of worms	starting or initiating something that will have negative consequences
opening old wounds	restarting or reinitiating something that will cause pain or conflict to someone else
out-foxed	out-smarted
out in left field	really misled or mistaken following the wrong lead
out of hide	without pay
out of reach	not attainable
out of sight...out of mind	if not reminded one tends to forget
out of the blue	from nowhere
out of the fryin' pan and into the fire	someone goes from one bad situation to a worse situation
out of the mouths of babes	This says that from the comments of children who are innocent and honest comes truth and wisdom
out of touch	not in contact with or knowledgeable of

out runnin' around	making rounds to various people and places
out to lunch	totally unrealistic
over a barrel	put in a difficult situation where one is required to act against their wishes
over-dressed	dressed inappropriate for situation in too formal attire
over the hill	old
over yonder	in that place where you are directed

P [85]

packin' a rod	carrying a gun on your person
paddle your own canoe	do your own work and attend to your own problems or issues
paint the town red	have a grand party or social event with others usually a wild time involving liquor
paintin' yourself in a corner	act in a manner to trap yourself in a situation where you have no way out
pallet	a crude makeshift bed
panty waste	a weak male
parts hanger	This term refers to someone working on an automobile where they just replace parts rather that repairing the parts.

Story from Then... *"Parts Hanger"* Harry Rogers Slaughter
It is literally unheard of for an automotive dealership or service center to "repair" a part today. My Grandfather Harry Rogers Slaughter was a

true mechanic. He was a mechanic during the Great Depression. I remember his basement workshop at his home. He saved everything including automotive parts and old electrical motors. He removed parts from automobiles and fixed or repaired them. He called others that couldn't do this "parts hangers". My grandfather worked for the government training soldiers in electrical and mechanical engineering during World War II at Ft. Campbell Military Base in Kentucky. When he retired as an automobile mechanic, he took a position at Ft. Campbell Laundry on the military installation. He was the overall engineer of all the automated machines in the large laundry. During that time, he developed three mechanical devices that were installed on the machines to improve performance or safety for the workers. He received awards from the military for these devices and they were patented with the United States Government. He also said that the ruin of the American Nation would be the philosophy of the "disposable pen". I often think of this when we find it less costly to buy a new appliance rather than have old appliance repaired. My grandfather had only an elementary school education through grade six because at that time he grew up he was needed to work on the farm and in the family country store in St. Bethlehem, Clarksville, Tn. and did not attend school.

party pooper	a no fun person at a party or in a social gathering
pass the buck	pass the blame for something to another
passing fancy,	a temporary amusement or enjoyment
paste board box	a box made of cardboard paper and glued or pasted together
pay your dues	put in your time to achieve status in a job or social position
peddle your own bicycle	take care of your own responsibilities and business

penny wise and a pound foolish	This term means stingy about small expenditures and extravagant with large ones.
pepper pot	hot tempered
pert near	near or close to
pickin' and grinnin'	When we gather socially with individuals who play different musical instruments, we have a *pickin' and grinnin'* session playing songs and singing. The instruments include guitars, banjos, autoharps, fiddles, and mandolins.

Story from Then... *"Pickin' and Grinnin'"* The Slaughter Family

Music is one of the most powerful elements of culture in my opinion. Our folk songs and spirituals carry stories and information that adds to the richness of the fabric of our civilization. The Slaughter side of my family, my mother's family, all had musical talents and played multiple instruments. They all sung three-part harmony socially and in church. Some family members could read music but my grandmother and other played strictly "by ear". This means the replicated the song based on their hearing it and not on reading printed notes on a sheet of music. The entire family usually gathered on the weekends at my Grandparents (Harry and Gertrude Slaughter) in Clarksville. After dinner we went to the drawing room at the front of the house and played and sung for hours. I grew up thinking that all families did such. As adults my sister and I play twelve string guitars. We have had a family and friend group that includes banjo, autoharp, twelve and six string guitars and a mandolin. Our collection of songs includes some 150 pieces. Some of the music is folk and some spiritual. There is nothing better than making a pot of homemade soup and sitting around the kitchen table pickin' and grinnin'.

Slaughter Family at 114 Marion Street Clarksville, Tennessee

pick-up truck	a regular sized truck with a bed for hauling
pickin' geese	pulling the feathers off a goose to make pillows or mattresses
pie-eyed	facial expression with eyes wide open
pigheaded	stubborn or obstinate
pig in a poke	somewhat of a sure thing "already in the bag'
piddle around	work or act aimlessly involved in unimportant activities
plain as the nose on your face	plain to see
plain Jane	simple with no special qualities or looks
plain mean	simply mean
plain slow	simply slow
plant a seed	give someone an idea that may lead to an action on their part
play your cards well	make good decisions
playin' 'possum	pretending as an opossum will lay on the ground and not move pretending to be dead to evade fighting conflicts
playin' hookie	skipping school or work without a valid reason or notifying your teacher or boss
playin' it cool	being calm
playin' your trump card,	the trump card is the winning card in a game of spades. *Trump card* comes from an old card game

called "triumph," shortened to just *trump* in the 1500's.

Source: Vocabulary.com

playing a game of cat and mouse participating in a dialogue with an opponent in a give and take situation

playing the field dating various people and not committing to just one individual

pleased as punch very pleased

plumb awful simply awful

plumb simply pretty

plumb right exactly right

plumb tuckered out very tired

polluted drunk

poor as a church mouse destitute and completely out of financial funds

poor as a turnip very poor

poor house a government-run facility to support and provide housing for the dependent or needy

Source: Wikipedia

pop a cork open a beverage especially a beer

poppin' your gum, a smacking noise that you make when you chew gum and blow bubbles

potluck meal with a potluck meal your meal is what is readily available or comes together from a variety of sources such as a "potluck" event social gathering where everyone brings a dish without planning with others. At church growing up we had a "potluck" about once a month for this reason or that. I was amazing to me that without prior planning or signing up for certain dishes adequate meats, vegetable dishes, breads and desserts arrived on the long wooden tables that we had set up in the fellowship hall of Forest Street United Methodist Church in Clarksville, Tennessee.

pray tell do tell me

precious cargo someone riding with you in the car you are driving

preachin' to the choir Individuals in the choir of a church are more likely to share the same convictions and opinions of the pastor or preacher. Preaching to the choir means trying to convince those who likely have the same opinion that you do.

pretty as a picture very pretty

pretty as a speckled pup very pretty

pretty is as pretty does	a person can be physically attractive yet act in a manner that is unattractive
pretty penny	a lot of money
prickly as a pear	very prickly
pride goes before a fall	everyone will fall at some point and a proud nature will eventually be compromised
prissy pants	very prudish
promises made to be broken	everyone changes their mind sometime
proud as a peacock	very proud
proud as punch	very proud
puckerin' up for a kiss	assuming the facial expression of the mouth and eyes as if in expecting a kiss
puffing like a steam engine	breathing with difficulty
pull my leg	joking me or fibbing as a joke
pull up your socks and blow your nose	be responsible and deal with your problems
pullin' his wait	doing your part or living up to your responsibilities
punchin' a time clock	This means keeping up with your work hours specifically without variance. A time clock is sometimes required at a working establishment where one uses a card to clock in and out.
puppy love	thinking you are in love at a very young age when you are probably infatuated

push comes to shove	things or circumstances in a situation accelerate
push your luck	pressing ahead too hard when you know your actions will be negative and risky
pushed to your limit	patience is really tried
pushin' up daisies	dead and buried
put back a little for a rainy day	saving something
put him six feet under	as in bury him under six feet of dirt
put it on the cuff	give me credit or charge it to me
put on the dog	behave in a pretentious manner
put on the back burner	delay action on
put on your knockabouts	work or casual clothes
put out	exasperated
put the hurt on him	cause him pain of some kind
put the kettle on	heat water for tea or coffee
put the pedal to the metal	press down on the accelerator of a vehicle to speed
put your two cents in	add a very insignificant comment not worth very much
puttin' on airs	acting pretentious or arrogant
puttin' on the dog	being pretentious
puttin' your best foot forward	giving something your best effort

Q [6]

quick on the draw	very anxious or ready

quiet as a buggy whip factory	It doesn't make much noise manufacturing buggy whips and whips are no longer used so the manufacture of them would not be a thriving enterprise.
quiet as a mouse	silent
quiet water runs deep	sometimes a person does not have to be outright and vocal to have deep thoughts
quit acting a fool	acting stupid
quit your preachin' and gone to meddlin'	you have overstepped in what you said going from providing a conversational reaction to being rude and insulting

R [83]

raidin' the refrigerator	getting something between meals out of the refrigerator
rainin' pitchforks	raining heavily
raining cats and dogs	raining heavily
raisin' Cain	causing a great disturbance
raising hell	causing a ruckus
ran like a scalded dog	ran fast
ran 'til his tongue hung outran	until he was exhausted
raspy throat	sore throat
rather lie than tell the truth	is so used to lying that it has become very comfortable
rattletrap	old broken down and junky automobile

rattlin' on and on	talking on and on without purpose
ready to rock and roll	ready to get started
ready to talk turkey	ready to seriously talk
red as a beet	very red
red headed as a peckerwood	very red
red hot	very hot
refresh your memory	remind you or give you the information again
remember...hell, yes	remember the War Between the States
restless as the wind	restless and swaying greatly in actions
rich old coot	old rich man
ridin' high in the saddle	doing very well
ridin' in the fast lane	doing very well
ridin' old Beck and leadin' old Maude'	riding one mule and leading the other means not making great progress but rather holding your own
ridin' shot gun	riding shotgun was used to describe the guard who rode alongside a stagecoach driver
right as rain	a person is perfectly fit and in superior physical health
right hand doesn't know what the left hand is doing	a person doesn't know what they are doing
right on the nose	correct
right smack dab in the middle	in the center of
ring in his nose	he is controlled by his wife like a bull being controlled by a ring in its nose
ring-tailed tooter	a mischievous individual

Source: Urban Dictionary

rip snorting headache	an extreme headache
rip-snortin' fight	a bad fight
ripe as a watermelon	very ripe
rise and shine	wake up from sleep
road hog	person taking up more lanes on a highway that allowed
road to destruction	person is on a self-destructive path
Robbin' Peter to pay Paul	borrowing funds here to pay a bill or debt there
rock the boat	to cause trouble or disturb a situation
rode hard- and put-up wet	woman looks used up and in poor condition
rollin' in the hay	love making
roof over my head	have a house to live in
rooked him out of his money	cheated him
room so small you can't change your mind	tiny room
rooted out of my warm place	took over my position
rosy as a peach	very pink
rotten to the core	completely bad or evil
rough as a cob	very rough as in rough as a corn cob
rough housin'	rough play indoors
rougher than a bull in a china shop	clumsy and not graceful
round as a butter ball	very rotund
round up	gather individuals or items as in a round up if cattle
rovin' eye	someone interested in looking for other partners of a sexual nature
rubbed her the wrong way	upset her
rubbed out	erased

rubber	a rubber band used to bind things together
ruckus	a commotion or disturbance
rule of thumb	the correct or prudent rule to go by
run by the store	drive to the store in the car
run downtown	drive down in the car
run like a deer	swiftly
run like the dickens swiftly	
runnin' a little late	running behind a planned or confirmed time or late for an appointment or completion of a task
runnin' around	go here and there without much necessity or planning
runnin' around like a chicken with its head cut off	This saying means running aimlessly around. When a chicken is slaughtered with its head being removed it will still run about the barnyard for several minutes.
runnin' behind time	running later that planned or confirmed
runnin' for office	politically campaigning
runnin' low	running at a low rate or at the level of deficiency
runnin' my tires off	traveling by automobile excessively
runnin' my wheels off	traveling by automobile excessively
runnin' myself ragged	wearing yourself out either physically or emotionally

runnin' off at the mouth	talking constantly without really thinking about what you are saying nor caring about how you are perceived
runnin' on borrowed time	you are out of time
runnin' on fumes	almost out if gasoline for your vehicle
runnin' out of steam	running out of energy
runnin' out of time	behind the planned timeline with an effort and feeling pressured to perform or act with more expedience
runnin' scared	afraid
runnin' 'til your tongue hangs out	working or performing until you are weary emotionally or physically
runnin' to keep up	acting or performing behind and trying to catch up
runnin' wild	acting without governance or behaving erratically and in a socially unacceptable manner
runny nose	nasal drainage
runs like a Cadillac	runs or operates very smoothly or efficiently
runs like a scared rabbit	runs very fast
runs like a well-oiled machine	works well with precision

S [258]

sacked out	gone soundly to sleep
sal hepatica	This is a mineral salt laxative that was produced and marketed by Bristol-

Myers from its inception in 1887, becoming its first nationally recognized product in 1903, until 1958. When dissolved in water, it was said to reproduce the taste and effect of the natural mineral waters of Bohemia.

Saturday Night Special

this a term used for a low quality inexpensive, compact, and small-caliber handgun

Story from Then… *"Saturday Night Special"* Charles Willard Slayden

My father is Charles Willard Slayden. He was what ne would call "a man's man". He had traditional values and was a patriotic and dedicated man to God, Family, and country. He was born in 1923 and lived well into his nineties. My father served in the Army Corps of Engineers in the Pacific Theatre during WWI. When he returned from the war he went to work with my grandfather and his brother in the building trades. He was a very good draftsman and drew the blueprints for all the structures that the company would build. My family would give a cost estimate for a build and then stand by their estimate not increasing it even if they went over budget. Any home that they built was designed and constructed with the philosophy it would be build it as if they were going to live in it themselves. When I was twelve years old my father had an accident at work that required him to transition from the physical demands of construction to another career. He became a policeman. My father earned his place through time rising through the ranks from a patrolman to the Chief of Police. My father was a brave man and would not send one of his subordinates to a situation that he wouldn't respond to himself. He was known by his men and women as a supportive and caring leader. He led by example through hard circumstances and times in Clarksville. His leadership style was a humanistic approach to dealing with people. He liked "putting opportunities before his officers that would give them a chance to develop or demonstrate skills and potential advancing their careers or contributions to the community. My father was my role model as a leader. As Chair of the Department of Teaching and Learning in the College of Education at Austin Peay State University I used his philosophy and advice on many matters. I aspired to have his skill and respect as a leader. My father's favorite quote was from Theodore Roosevelt and the piece entitled "The Man in the Arena" was framed on the wall of his office. My father was a Man's Man and one to be admired, respected, and loved.

sauce for the goose is sauce for the gander

what is good for one person in a particular circumstance or situation is also good for another in the same circumstance or situation

sawing logs

snoring

scalawag

In United States history, scalawags (sometimes spelled scallawags or scallywags) were white Southerners who supported Reconstruction after the American Civil War.

Source: Wikipedia

scaldin' hot

extremely hot liquid

scapegoat

With origins in Biblical times and roots in the Jewish tradition, a scapegoat is one who bears the blame for others, wrongly.

scarce as hen's teeth

it doesn't get any scarcer than this because chicken don't have teeth

scared out of your wits

so scared that you can't think straight

scared stiff

so scared that you feel unable to act

scared the hell out of me

to shock or frighten someone severely and suddenly

142

scared to death	so scared that you fear a heart attack
scaredy cat	afraid in an irrational way
scratch my back and I'll scratch yours	take care of me by doing favors for me and I will return the favor
screaming like a wildcat	screaming or screeching wildly
scuttlebutt	This is a slang term for rumor or gossip. The term comes from a similar situation comparable to a water cooler in an office setting today. In the days of great sailing ships water for immediate consumption was conventionally stored in a scuttled butt: a butt or a cask which had been scuttled by making a hole in it so the water could be withdrawn. Since sailors exchanged gossip when they gathered at the scuttlebutt for a drink of water, scuttlebutt became Navy slang for gossip or rumors.

Source: Wikipedia

screwier than a squirrel	crazy or erratic
second-class citizen	This term refers to a person being treated unequally or in a

disrespectful manner. Second class citizens originally were individuals belonging to a social or political group whose rights and opportunities are inferior to those of the dominant group in a society. At one time women had been denied the vote and been made into second-class citizens.

second hand	used or recycled
see you if the creeks don't rise	water doesn't overflow the road
seein' dollar signs	anticipating wealth
seein' each other	keeping company or dating
seein' is believin'	person would have to see something to believe it
self-educated	educated through one's own efforts and not by formal instruction

Story from Then... *"Self-Educated"* Willie Alma Baker Slayden

My paternal grandmother was Willie Alma Baker Slayden. She married my grandfather, her elder of fourteen years, when she was seventeen years old. She had three sons and was a faithful Methodist church woman. Currently almost all women were homemakers and did not work outside of the home. My grandmother was an excellent seamstress and fantastic cook. She gardened and did most of the yardwork in addition to taking care of domestic duties and rearing children. I can remember spending countless hours with her during summer afternoons when she read to me, or we went on nature walks. She was the first environmentalist that I knew. She was a naturalist as well. We explored creeks and woods and watched birds. We collected and identified butterflies and moths. At night we did star study on a pallet in her front yard. She was an avid reader focusing on non-fiction and natural science and history. The National Geographic Magazine became my portal to the outside world, and I listened to reports and analysis of readings during each month while she awaited the next issue. My first "official card" was my library card to the Clarksville-Montgomery County Library. During summer afternoons we would spend countless hours there always coming home with the treasured five books on loan for one week. My grandmother was good friends with the librarian and told me that my grandmother had read practically all the works on nature and history. Well into her eighties we still took hikes and looked for fossils. She taught me a love for the written word. She once said, "close your eyes as I read and see the picture in your mind". This was a time with limited black and white television and no internet. My grandmother was the President of the Women's' Society of Forest Street United Methodist Church in Clarksville. She taught Bible study and Sunday school every year that I can remember. She was a good researcher using multiple reference sources and documentations to prepare her lessons. My grandmother was an excellent conversationalist and could participate in any dialog with family and friends. She was valued and respected as a very intelligent and learned person. She was self-taught or self-educated. I learned to love study and teaching from her.

separate the wheat from the chaff	examine what is good and bad or correct and incorrect
set a spell	sit and visit for awhile
set sail	embark or set out on a venture
settin' up house keepin'	following marriage a couple moves in together to live together and they combine their resources and begin a life as a couple including organizing the household
set your heart	decided irrevocably that you want something
set your mind	make a firm decision that you are going to do something
set your mind at ease	relieve your worries
settin' yourself up	positioning yourself
settle up with you later	will pay or reimburse you for something later
settlin' in	settling down
settlin' in for the night	getting ready for the evening
sewin' wild oats	to engage in premarital flings with numerous sexual partners or to spread one's genes around by impregnating many females
shacked up	living together as man and wife and not married
shade tree mechanic	This term refers to someone who is doing mechanical work as a lay

person. Typically, in the south men would work in their yard and use a large limb of a tree to hoist the engine from vehicle. This is where my male relatives did most of the work on our automobiles. Currently engines were simpler with no computers and sensors and were much easier to work on.

shady character	a person who is not trustworthy or reliable and has the potential for unlawful behavior
shady deal	a deal that is questionable and possible unlawful
sharp	smart
sharp as a mother in laws tongue	pointed and brassy in a negative and condemning manner
sharp as a razor	very sharp
sharp as a tack	very sharp
sharp as a whip	very sharp
she chickened out	she became intimidated and afraid to act
she gave him his walkin' paper	she broke up with him or gave him his divorce papers

she gave him the brush off	she ignored him
she has him on a downhill drag	she has conquered him
she has him wrapped around her little finger	she has him doing everything and anything she desires
she holds the purse strings	controls the finances and money
shenigans	secret or dishonest activity or maneuvering
she is plain stuck up	arrogant and pious
she is the spittin' image of her mom	looks just like her mom
she let him down	she disappointed him
she makes him walk the chalk line	she monitors his behavior keeping him on the straight and narrow path
she really puts on feedbag	she serves a good meal
she sure has a cool head	she is collected and able to thing about thins rationally
she turned her nose up to the meal	she didn't like the meal or thought that the food was inappropriate
she two-timed him	dated someone else at the same time she was dating him
she's a cracker jack	great person
she's a good old soul	good individual
she's a hussy	promiscuous person
she's a thorn in my side	she is an irritation to me
she's an old stick in the mud	she is resistant and prudish
she's been spoken for	she is engaged
she's flipped her wig	she's become irrational
she's in a family way	she is pregnant
she's like watered down buttermilk	she is weak and not genuine

she's money hungry	she craves a large amount of money, or her desires are mostly for things of monetary value
she's not as big as a washin' of soap	she is a person of small statue
she's set her cap for him	she has decided that she wants him
she's settin' her head for him	she has decided that she wants him
she's sulled up	she is pouting
shifty	not trustworthy and unreliable
shoddy	poorly or cheaply made as in something of poor quality
shoo the flies off the table	wave your hands over the table and frighten away the flies
shootin' off your mouth	talking without thinking about what you are saying or the consequences for what you say
shoppin' for vittles	shopping for groceries
short and sweet, pleasant	by brief
shortly	before long
shot gun wedding	wedding of necessity because the bride is pregnant, and marriage is the honorable and expected outcome
show off	acting out
showed himself	showed his real character without inhibitions
sick and tired	totally tired of something

sick as a dog

This idiom means very ill. A dog was considered an undesirable animal in the 17th century. So much so that there are a lot of phrases which refer to them negatively [tired as a dog, dog in the manger, down to the dogs, dog's breakfast, dirty dog, etc.]. Sick as dog refers to being so sick that one may feel like vomiting. The first literary use of the expression is in 1705.

(The Idioms: Largest Idioms Dictionary, 2021)

sidetracked	off task the saying comes from trains that have sidetracks
silly as a goose	extremely silly or foolish
silly willy	extremely silly or foolish
sing like a bird	singing beautifully
singin' harmony	singing third part harmony with someone
singin' like a stool pigeon	person acting as a whistleblower
sink like a rock	sink immediately because rocks don't float
sittin' in the catbird's seat	in a very advantageous position
sittin' in the driver's seat	in a very advantageous position

sittin' in the front room	sitting in the parlor or living room of someone's house
sittin' on pins and needles	nervous
sittin' pretty	in a very advantageous position
sittin' there like a knot on a log	sitting and not responding
six of one and half a dozen of the other	either option is the same and equal
skatin' on thin ice	in a tenuous or potentially dangerous position
skeleton in the closet	something you would rather people not know about you
skidded to a halt	stopped by locking the breaks and skidding to a stop
skillet-lickin' good	so tasty one would be tempted to lick the skillet for the last taste of something
skin like an alligator	rough skin
skinny as a rail	extremely thin and frail
skinny as a bean pole	This comparison means extremely thin and frail as in a "bean pole". Typically, thin poles are driven in the ground in a garden as a trellis for the growing bean plants.
skinny dippin'	swimming naked
skippin' out	leaving without telling others that you are going potentially shirking a duty or avoiding doing

	something that you should do prior to leaving
skippin' school	not going to school for no good reason
slap the fun out of you	person looked as if he had been slapped and if he had been slapped, he would have immediately changed his facial expression from a jovial mood to one of surprise or anger
slap you cock eyed	slapped or knocked so that your eyes cross
sleep like a log	sleep very soundly
sleep tight don't let the bed bugs bite	have a good night's sleep
sleepin' like a log	sleeping soundly
slick as a whistle	sharp or impressive
slick as an eel	very ingenious in a sneaky way
slick as an onion	very ingenious in a sneaky way
slicker as snot	very slick
slime ball	a bad or incredulous person
slingin' mud	name calling
slip of the tongue	information given that should have been reserved or privileged
slipped a stitch	forgot something
slippery than wet glass	quite slippery
Sloan's Liniment	This is a liniment that temporarily relieves aches and pains of muscles or pains due to arthritis. The Sloan family emigrated from Ireland in the early

	nineteenth century.(Drugs.com, 2021)
sloppin' the hogs	feeding the hogs with slop that is slushy liquid food waste
slow and steady wins the race	be steady and constant without wavering to accomplish a task
slow as a snail	exceptionally slow
slow as Christmas	exceptionally slow
slow as molasses	exceptionally slow
slower than a three-legged mule	exceptionally slow
slowin' down to a screachin' halt	slowing down to a point of an abrupt stop
slowly but surely,	it may take time, but it will happen without question
sly as a fox	This idiom means very cunning. In the ancient mythology and in numerous European and East Asian folklore, foxes were considered sacred animals.
smack dab	right on or exactly on top of or in an exact spot
small as a flea	tiny
small fry	a small or immature child or fish
smart aleck	This idiom refers to one who is given to obnoxious and insolent humor. This individual is pretentious and obnoxiously self-assured.
smellin' like a rose	smelling of perfume and sweet scent

smells like a five and ten cent store

This means smelling of perfume and sweet scent. Five and ten cent stores were the fore runners of stores like Walmart. They were variety stores on a much smaller scale.

smile like a ray of sunshine

a moment of enlightenment or encouragement providing hope

smoke house

an outdoor structure where harvested pork in the form of hams and sausage were hung on wood racks above a slow burning fire to "smoke" the meat

smokin' like a smokestack

heavy smoker of tobacco or cigarettes

smokin' up a storm

smoking greatly

smooth as silk

very smooth

smooth sailing

wishing one good fortune

snake in the grass

a sneaky individual

snake oil

Snake oil is a euphemism for deceptive marketing. It refers to the petroleum-based mineral oil or "snake oil" that used to be sold as a cure-all elixir for many kinds of physiological problems. Many 19th-century United States and 18th-century European entrepreneurs advertised and sold mineral oil. It was often mixed with various active and inactive household herbs, spices, and compounds but containing no snake-derived substances whatsoever.

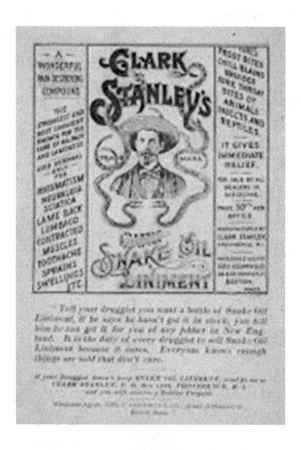

Snake Oil (The Tribune, 2021)

snap out of it	come out of it
sneaky as a snake	very sneaky
snug as a bug in a rug	warm and comfortable
so buck-toothed she could chew	

corn through a picket fence

extreme dental problems having protruded upper teeth

so busy I meet myself coming back
so tired he was ready to drop
socked him
sock money away

turning in all directions
physically exhausted
hit him
save money as in saving it in "a sock"

so cold it'd freeze the balls off a brass monkey

The original "Brass Monkey" was a brass platform or plate used to store iron cannonballs in the 16th and 18th centuries.

The Monkey had small indentations to stop the balls rolling about, and when stacked the balls formed a pyramid. The plates had indentions in them that held the balls on the bottoms of the stacks which were stacked in a pyramid shape. Brass, however, expands and contracts with the temperature and if it got cold enough, the cannon balls could fall...giving real foundation to the phrase "cold enough to freeze the balls off a brass monkey!"

Source: Truth or Fiction

**so cross-eyed when she cries
tears roll down her back**   extremely cross eyed or affected by Strabismus

so fat he must hug her one side at a time   obese person is the object of affection

so flop-eared he looks like a cab with both doors open   ears standing out from both sides of his head

so lazy he wouldn't hit a lick at a snake so lazy he wouldn't lift a stick to kill a snake

so mad he's about to blow a fuse This means very angry. Most homes built after 1965, as well as older homes that have updated electrical services, have circuit breakers that control the electrical circuits in their homes. In older homes the electrical circuits are protected and controlled by fuses located in a central fuse box. These devices serve the same function as circuit breakers to protect against circuit overloads and short circuits. Unlike circuit breakers you can't reset them. They simply become overheated to the point that they burn or blow out as in "Blowing a fuse".

Source: The Free Dictionary by Farlex

so mad he blew a gasket   This means to become very angry or upset and to figuratively cause a seal or gasket to fail. A gasket is any mechanical seal that fills the space between two objects to prevent leakage while under compression. This refers to the head gasket on an automobile.

Source: Wiktionary

so mean the devil wouldn't have him	meanest of the mean
so quiet you could hear a rat pee on cotton	completely silent
so sick she can't hold her head up	extremely ill
so skinny he could hide behind a clothesline	very thin and could hide behind an outdoor cotton cord hung to dry clothes
so slow he met himself comin' back	making no progress at all
so slow you are goin' backwards	very, very slow
so spoiled he stinks	so spoiled that he is like rotten food
so thick you can't stir 'em with a stick	extremely crowded together
so tight that they squeak	tight as in stingy with money
so ugly only his mother could love him	the ugliest of the ugly
soft as a baby's bottom	very soft
soft as butter	very soft
somebody must have dropped the set out of their ring	a loud noise is heard
sometimes I think my git up and go got up and went	I think that all my energy is gone
sore loser	resentful for losing
sorry as sorry can be	as sorry as a person can be about something

sorry so and so	a sorry or bad person that you might add other adjectives to as in so...and so...
soul searching	being introspective and self-evaluative
sound like a broken record	a vinyl record with a crack in it jumps and repeats itself over and over
sounds like a $2 radio	cheap sound system or a sound like radio static which is worrisome
soup line	People lined up daily for free soup or food during the Great Depression.

(U-S-History.com, 2021)

sour grapes	a person holding a grudge
sour puss	person with a sour facial expression specifically

	with a puckered mouth in a pouting expression
soused	drunk
sow belly and turnip greens	turnip greens cooked with or seasoned with pork
spanked 'til you can't sit down	a child paddled or spanked to the point of having his/her posterior made sore so that sitting would be temporarily painful
spare the rod and spoil the child	do not hesitate to correct your child for inappropriate behavior and that includes corporal punishment like spanking
sparkin'	courting, dating, or keeping company
speak of the devil	This phrase is used to acknowledge the coincidence of someone arriving at a scene just at the time that they are being talked about. museum of London
Speaks volumes	says a lot or conveys much information
spend the night and we'll hang you on a nail	this is a joke saying that we have no sleeping accommodations, but we will hang you on a nail where the coast or hats hang
spendin' money like it's goin' out of style	spending money so rapidly that it looks as if you think

	it might be something that would go out of style
spicket	a faucet

Note: 6.38% of the people in the US use the term spicket or spigot to refer to a faucet or tap that water comes out of

Source: Vocabulary.com

spinning your wheels	making no progress or going nowhere as in the spinning wheels of a car
spittin' image	looks exactly like someone
splitin' hairs	being extremely particular
splittin' headache,	a headache so severe that it makes your head feel like it is splitting open
spoiled brat	a spoiled child or offspring
spring fever	an anxious, restless, or eager feeling with the onslaught of spring weather
spring house	a small wooden structure built over or around a natural spring that emerges from the ground
squawk box	a radio
squealin' like a stuck pig	shrieking or squealing loudly as a pig that has had its throat cut during slaughter
squeeze box	an accordion
stallin' for time	procrastinating
stand up to them	stand up for yourself
standin' in the need of prayer	needing spiritual help
standin' my ground	not wavering

stark raving mad

truly insane or crazy

stay away from him...it'll rub off on you

if you associate with him, he may sway or persuade you in a negative way

stay in my right mind

maintain my ability to think clearly and logically

stayin' in the groove

staying on track

step on a crack and break your mother's back

This is an old children's game, anyone who trod on the cracks between the paving stones was out, until only one player was left, he or she was then declared the winner. Most of us know the old rhyme *"Step on a crack, break your mother's back."* Whether the rhyme is the cause of, or a result of, this superstition is uncertain, though belief in it persists in many people today, even if subconsciously. Come to think of it, avoiding sidewalk cracks is probably a good policy for anyone who wants to avoid tripping.

Source: Urban Dictionary

step-ins

These are a type of slip-on women's underwear that resembles men's boxer shorts.

Step-ins. (Museum of London, 2021)

steppin' on someone's toes	insulting someone
stick in the mud	a contrary person
stick to your guns	hold your position and don't compromise
stick to your ribs	something that you eat that seems to make you feel satisfied for a long time
sticks and stones may break bones, but names will never hurt me	what a person says about you will not actually physically harm you

still wet behind the ears	young and naïve as when one was just born
stirrin' up a stink	this means beginning to start or perpetuate something that is going to cause a problem like causing something to smell worse by stiring it
stole my heart	caused me to love you and commit my heart to you
stole my thunder	use another's idea to an advantage
stone deaf	totally deaf
stoned drunk	
stop off on the way in	stopped or paused by to see someone or go somewhere on the way into this place
straddlin' a barbed wire fence	in a difficult position
straddlin' the fence	not sure about how you feel about an issue
strap my razor	This saying means to sharpen my razor or get me ready to face a situation. Straight razors were sharpened by rubbing them on a leather strap called a razor strap.

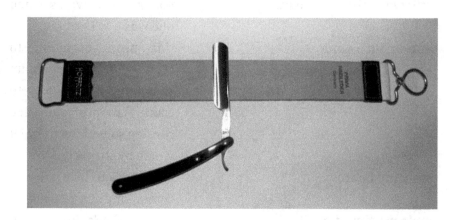

straw that broke the camel's back

the last thing that really verified that nothing more could be tolerated as in the very greatest load that a camel could carry and not one straw more

strike while the iron is hot

This saying means act on an opportunity while the conditions are favorable. This saying likely comes from wordage regarding metallurgy and blacksmithing. It would imply striking a hot piece of metal with a mallet or tool before it cools so that it could be shaped.

(Google Dictionary, 2021)

string along

reluctantly accompany someone

stripped a gear

changed directions in behavior completely and instantly

strippin' your gears	changing your mind so quickly that it is like changing the gears of a standard shift car without pushing in the clutch which would break or strip the gears in the transmission of the automobile
strong as an ox	very strong
struck it rich	became rich is a comparison of a person to a prospector digging with a pick striking rock and mineral that would make him rich
struck out on the first date	made a bad impression
struttin' around like a banty rooster	means a small person behaving in a belligerent manner like a banty rooster is a small rooster struts around the coop wooing the hens
struttin' your stuff	walking proudly
stubborn as a mule	very stubborn and referred to being "long headed" as in the shape of a mule's head
stumped	completely confused
stylin'	showing great style and flare
such a turned-up nose she would drown in the rain	a snooty person or
arrogant person	
Sunday goes to meetin' clothes	dress clothes or ones that you would wear to church on Sunday
sure, as I'm born	for certain

sure nuff	sure enough or for certain
swallow your pride	give up being prideful
swamp cabbage	the cabbage-like terminal bud has been eaten as hearts of palm. The growing heart of the new fronds gives the tree its "cabbage" name, since this is extracted as a food and tastes like other undifferentiated plant meristem tissue, such as the heart of a cabbage or artichoke.

The bristles on the sheaths of young leaves have been made into scrubbing brushes. The trunks have been used as wharf piles. On June 28, 1776, Charleston patriots under William Moultrie made a fort of palmetto trunks and from it defended successfully against the British in the Revolutionary War. The palm is a part of the South Carolina state flag for this reason.

Source: Wikipedia

Story from Then... *"Swamp Cabbage"* Arlie Mae Baker Wilder

When we went to visit my Great Aunt Arlie in Central Florida, in a town called Mount Dora, we would spend a lot of time outdoors. She was an outdoors person and loved natural science. At this time in Central Florida

Disney World had not been built. We would fish the lake and walk the woods finding gopher shells (shells from dead turtles). We would always find a swamp cabbage palm which we would cut down. That night we would have the delicious cabbage that was shredded and cooked with port seasoning Aunt Arlie's house was on Lake Joanna surrounded by acres of orange groves and citrus fruits on sand roads. As a young woman my aunt worked as the teacher in a one-room schoolhouse in Dixon County Tennessee. She later moved to Central Florida with other family members. Her family lived in an old three-story wood frame house on the lake during the time that she had three children. After her children started elementary school, she worked in a packing plant where she packed oranges by hand into wooden crates. This was during the time of The Great Depression. Her husband had a steady job as a barber but there was a scarcity of everything. Her work supplemented the family income, and she used any money left over to buy up land all around the lake for back taxes. She then planted acre after acre of citrus fruit. She did the disking with a Massey Ferguson tractor herself until the business grew to the extent that she hired pickers and trucks. Her husband. Claude passed away in his late forties. She managed the grove business by herself well into her late eighties. During the 1960s she decided that she would like to have a vacation house back in Tennessee. She bought a single-wide trailer and a couple of acres on the side of a mountain in the Smoky Mountains. She hired a contractor to relocate the trailer. He was glad to help her but insisted, "you know Mrs. Wilder there is no road up that mountain". She replied to him "well then I guess you will have to build one". He did and then hooked the trailer to his bulldozer and took the trailer up the side of that mountain and set it on its new foundation. I spent vacation time there with her in a situation where "time had been turned back to the old times". We had electricity and well water but no hot water. She did not allow a television in her house, but we always entertained ourselves by reading, walking, and talking telling stories about yester year. Later she had a small wood house on Barton's Creek in Dickson County. She bought a house on the creek close to the location where she grew up. Her favorite possession was the Massey Ferguson tractor. She hired crews of men to do the disking of the citrus groves, but she never stopped riding her tractor and doing light work. In her later years she had to replace her refrigerator and the old one was placed on her carport. She asked her son and grandsons to take it off four or five times. After a period of a couple of weeks the grandsons went by to check about helping with the refrigerator and it wasn't there. They ask her what happened to it, and she replied, "you were busy, so I took care of it myself". She told them that she dug a large hole in her back yard with the tractor and buried the refrigerator. She was a most independent and resourceful person. She is the only self-actualized person I have ever known. She was completely satisfied with life and passionate about all aspects of it. She was a school mistress in a one room schoolhouse in Tennessee. She was an exceptional artist using a variety of mediums including pencil and paints. My Aunt Arlie, like her sister, my grandmother Willie, was well read and very much a naturalist. At her death she was a wealthy woman but still had her tractor. I now have an ignition key to her tractor that I treasure.

Arlie Mae Baker Wilder

sweat of your brow If you earn money that you use to live on it is "by the sweat of your brow" meaning that it is by doing hard physical work. This term originates from the Bible (Romans 5:12-21):

Story from Then... *"Sweat of Your Brow"* Charles Alvin Slayden

My paternal grandfather was Charles Alvin Slayden. He was a giant of a man but had a heart of gold. He was one of fourteen children and grew up on a farm in Dickson County. The farm life required planting cash crops, an extensive garden, and raising a large variety of farm animals. This life sustained the large family and they either grew or made everything they need to exist and thrive in this rural environment. My grandfather also learned the trade of carpentry. During the Great Depression when my grandparents had three sons to raise not many people had any money at all and building trades all but ceased. My father remembered his father working at the rail yard moving railroad cars with long iron poles with twenty or thirty other men for fifty cents a day. My grandfather would place his heavy wooden toolbox on his shoulder and walk all the way across town to repair a window for someone. After the Great Depression he prospered again. He was a master builder and eventually went into business with my father and uncles as a contractor in both Dickson and Clarksville, Tennessee and in Miami, Florida. They were contractors on the Homestead Airforce Base for the government and hotels on Miami Beach. My relatives were hard workers but more than that they had very high ethics. They build a home with the thought in mind that it would be done for the original estimate and that it would be a structure that any of them would be willing to live in. My male relatives could do anything and never hired anyone to do mechanical, electrical, plumbing, or building work. We had someone in the family that could do any kind of work.

Slayden Family: (Top Row Left to Right) Alvin, Woodroe, Lela, Ora.
(Second Row Left to Right) Eva, Della, Mary Eliza, Lela
(Bottom Row Left to Right) Odessa, Papa (Henry), Mama (Julia), Mable

Immediate Slayden Family Charles Alvin Slayden and Willie Alma Baker Slayden
(Top Left to Right) Henry Thomas and Charles Willard Slayden
(Bottom Left to Right) Willie, David Wesley, and Alvin
Note: Top Left Alvin Slayden in Army Uniform WWI France 1920

Henry Thomas Slayden	Charles Williard Slayden
sweet tooth	a person who really likes sweets
swimmin' in the raw	swimming naked

swimmin' up stream	trying to consistently work or fight for something making little progress
swims like a rock	can't swim
swingin' like a washwoman	on wash day the "washwoman" was usually in less than a great mood and prone to taking swings and swats at troublesome children. Women had to get up early on wash day and build a large fire that burned down to coals. She then placed a large kettle over the fire to boil and put lye soap in the water. The clothes were boiled, rinsed, wrung out, and hung on an outdoor clothesline to dry. There were no permanent press or new age materials for clothes. These were homemade clothes as well.

This process would perpetuate a less than "good mood".

swingin' your weight around	using your size or position to your advantage

T [153]

tag along	go along with
take a back seat	defer to someone else to move ahead or take precedence over yourself
take a load off	relieve someone

look around	go somewhere and visit around the place observing what you can see
take a nosedive	go headfirst
take a snort	take a drink
take care of your pennies and your dimes will take care of themselves	If you save pennies as well as dimes eventually the pennies will total up to the worth of dimes. This saying advocates the saving of all coins, and they will over time total a significant amount.
take 'em down a notch or two	refers to the tightening or loosening a belt with the holes or notches that are in the belt
take in the sidewalk	some towns are so small that in the evening you don't see anyone walking on the sidewalks as if they had been rolled up"
take it at face value	to accept someone or something as it appears
take it with a grain of salt	pay no attention to it
take no stock	have no belief in something
take time to smell the flowers	make time for important things in your life
take up for each other	look out for each other's interests...as in my brother's keeper
take your medicine like a man	be responsible and accept what is coming to you
talk is cheap	let me see something concrete

talkin' like a magpie	talks too much or constantly
talkin' out of both sides of your mouth	being two-faced or contradictory to yourself
talkin' out of turn	talking about something that you aren't familiar with in front of others who are well informed
talkin' to hear my head rattle	talking to just be talking and for no good purpose
talkin' up a storm	talking incessantly
tall in the saddle	has a good image
tattle tale	a gossip
tea towel	a dish cloth
teacher's pet	teacher's favorite student
teeth like piano keys	attractive teeth that are pearly white and straight
teeth like stars. they come out at night	false teeth
tell it to the judge	you will have your time in the future or in court so save that excuse for that time
tend to your own knittin'	mind your own business
tend to your own rat killin'	mind your own business
that dog won't hunt	that excuse won't work with me
that last step's a doozy	Coming from the 1800s, doozy originally meant something that is extraordinary. Doozy can also mean that something is troublesome or problematic.
that was a close shave	I came close

178

that was a hoot	that was something unusual and funny
that will be enough from the peanut gallery	that is all to be heard from a person of so little importance
that's a lost cause	something that can't be attained
that's gonna be a hard egg to crack	something very difficult to do
that's gonna be a tough nut to crack	something very difficult to do
that's it in a nutshell	here is the short version or summary
that's like the pot callin' the kettle black	All cast iron cookware is black. This cookware included kettles and cook pots of all sizes. This cookware is still made in modern times. This type of cookware was originally used on wood stoves or open fires. I still use my "Dutch Ovens" and large frying pans to cook vegetables and foods in because they cook at high temperatures well without sticking and are easy cleanup.
that's long gone	it is over with
that's the last straw	the last toleration
that's the way the chips fall	let something happen no matter the consequences

that's the way the cookie crumbles	that is just the way it happens
that's a laugh	an irony
the apple doesn't fall too far from the tree	an offspring is like his/her parents
the bigger they are the harder they fall	anyone can be defeated regardless of size or importance, position, or power
the cat's out of the bag	it is now known and not a secret or protected thing
the darkest hour is just before midnight	sometimes the hardest time is near the end
the end justifies the means	what is done warrants the action
the fat will be fryin' tonight	he will be in trouble tonight
the house smells musty	smells damp and of mold
the long and short of it	the complete summary
the more the merrier	a large number or more people are welcomed
the Old Grey Mare...she ain't what she used to be	she cannot perform in the same way as previously
The Prodigal Son	This refers to someone who is welcomed accepted regardless of their previous behavior. The Parable of the Prodigal Son is one of the parables of Jesus in the Bible and appears in Luke 15:11–32.

the South will rise again	reference to the Civil War or the War Between the States
the stork's goin' to fly	the couple will have a baby
the thorn in my side	a problem that I have
the umpire has rabbit ears	he is sensitive to comments
the whole ball of wax	everything
the whole kit and caboodle	this saying mean the whole lot
the whole nine yards	the entire amount
the worlds not goin' to stop spinnin'	this is not all important
there are more pebbles on the beach than one	you have options and have many individuals to choose from when looking for a mate
there is no earthly reason for it	no explainable reason or cause
there's no place like home	your home is your most comfortable place
they broke up	they are not together anymore
they live across the tracks	in a low-income area of the town or city
they pulled the rug out from under him	they unexpectedly surprised him
thick as thieves	very friendly and committed to ear other
thing-a-ma-jig	something you don't know the name for
things are lookin' up	my situation seems to be improving
thinks he's God's gift to women	thinks he is attractive to all the women

third wheel	three people sometimes make a crowd when just a couple would like to be alone and therefore a bicycle only needs "two wheels"
this case is all wrapped up	it is concluded
those scissors wouldn't cut hot butter	they are dull
three sheets to the wind	drunk
threw a party	gave a party and had guests
throwin' his weight around	exerting his authority too much or too freely
thrown for a loop	this means the same thing as "thrown a curve" meaning being surprised
thrown in the slammer	put in jail
thunderashuns!	exclamation of rage and hostility
thunder thighs	fat or chubby thighs
tickle box turned over	laughing uncontrollably
tickled pink	pleased
tie one on	the act of becoming intoxicated
tied down	definitely accomplished
tied up	encumbered
tighter than dick's hatband	very tight with money or stingy
'Til I can get a toe hold	until I can get established
'Til Hell freezes over	never

'Til the cows come home until it's all over

time caught up with him	he has finally been found out
time marches on	time keeps moving on and forward
time to tie the knot	time to get married
time will tell	we will see what happens
tip of the iceberg	just the beginning of something
tip the scales	cause something to go this way or that
toe sack	a burlap sack
toe the mark	follow the rules exactly
Tommy Rot nonsense	
tomorrow's another day	there is a future
tongue loose at both ends	talks too much telling everything
tongue twister	something difficult to say
tongue-waggin'	talking a lot
too big for your britches	acting arrogant and unrealistically capable
too close for comfort	something negative almost happened to me

too far gone	cannot be saved
too many cooks spoil the broth	there are leaders and followers and each is necessary, and everyone cannot be the leader or the "cook"
too many irons in the fire	too many things to do or too much on "your plate"
too smart for your own good	too informed
tootin' your own horn	bragging on yourself
top dog	top leader
toppin' tall cotton	The term "high cotton" or "tall cotton" originates from the rural farming community in the antebellum (pre-Civil War) South. This is when "high cotton" meant that the crops were good and the prices were, too. The term has generalized to mean one is doing well or is successful.

Source: Wiktionary

tote bag	a bag to carry thing in
tote the wood	carry the wood
tourist cabin	small cabins for rent for travelers prior to motels and hotels along travel roads and highways
track 'em down	follow a clue
traded a ring for a ball and chain	got married

treat me like a stepchild	treat me not as well as you would treat your own biological children
troublemaker	someone who instigates something negative or harmful
truck stop	a store where professional truckers frequent for fuel, food, and other needs
tryin' their wings	trying something for the first time
tryin' to get ahead	trying to make progress or succeed bettering yourself from your current position or condition
tryin' to get a toe hold	trying to achieve a vantage point or a posture to start something
tryin' to smooth it out	trying to make things right
tryin' to throw off a virus	trying to withstand and overcome being physically sick
trying to be something you're not	being pretentious and fake in your actions
trying to squirm out of it	trying to back paddle or work your way out of something with explanation and excuses
tucked his tail between his legs	retreated in shame or embarrassment
tune up and cry	it is easy to see that you are getting ready to cry
turn in	go to bed or retire for the night
turn on a dime	can turn sharply

turn on the heat	accelerate a situation and put more pressure on someone
turn over a new leaf	begin again
turn the other cheek	This saying urges the person wronged to give the person committing the wrong a second chance. Turn the other cheek is a phrase in Christian doctrine from the Sermon on the Mount that refers to responding to injury without revenge.
turn up like a bad penny	This saying means that a disreputable or unwanted event will always reoccur, and a proverb has existed since the ties of the Middle Ages implying that some coins were "bad" as in debased or counterfeit. The 'clipping' of coins was rife in the Middle Ages, long before standardization of the coinage was reliably enforced.

(The Free Dictionary by Farlex, 2021)

turn you every way but loose	an angry threat meaning that you will not be released
turn your love off like runnin' water	turn your love on and off

turnin' out a beard	growing a beard
turnip salat	turnip greens
twenty years if he's a day	he is at least twenty years old
twinkle toes	a person who is nimble and quick on their feet
two bag ugly	so ugly a person has two bags over their head...in case one bag gets a hole in it
two-bit lawyer	a cheap and ineffective lawyer that would cost a few dollars to employ
two cards short of a deck	not playing with a full deck or mentally incapable of proper performance
two-faced	dishonest or not to be trusted
two left feet	very clumsy
two peas in a pod	two things or individuals that are very much akin or just alike in someway
two shakes of a lamb's tail	would not take very long as lambs shake their tails constantly
two wrongs don't make a right	you cannot correct something by committing a second wrong, mistake or indiscretion
two's enough three's a plenty	three people in a situation make a crowd when the original two would prefer to be alone

U [15]

ugly as a barbed wire fence	extremely uncomely or unattractive
ugly as a brood sow	very ugly or visually unattractive
ugly as a cross-eyed mule	very ugly or visually unattractive
ugly as a mud fence	very ugly or visually unattractive
ugly as home-made sin	very ugly or visually unattractive
ugly as sin	very ugly or visually unattractive
under the table	payment unrecorded as "under the table leg" sometimes to avoid paying taxes
under the weather	feeling poorly or in poor health
unevenly yoked	the common reference compares a team of oxen saying that a well-paired team pulls well together. The saying comes from the Bible.

The Bible warns about individuals who are unevenly yoked: *2 Corinthians 6:14. The New International Version translation says, "Do not be unequally yoked together with unbelievers."*

Story From Then... *"Unevenly Yoked"* Ruby Jo Slaughter Slayden

My mother, Ruby Jo Slaughter Slayden, was one of the brightest and vigorous people that I have ever known. Her intelligence made her an interesting person and "my first and best teacher". Many of the idioms in this book come from her. She was a devoted parent and family member. She was a committed and involved Christian. My mother lived her faith and made daily examples of Christian living in practice. Mother told us frequently that we would be known by the company we kept and that we should associate and form relationships with those individuals who held our same ideals and beliefs. She offered advice to us on marriage. She told us that the Bible speaks of being "evenly yoked". This related to marriage and stresses that the two individuals should be of the "sameness of mind" and hold the same ideals and share the same philosophical viewpoints. The family is the greatest element of society and the marriage of two individuals is the founding of the family.

upset the apple cart	disturb or interrupt something
up start	a novice with little experience acting as if they are an experienced person who should take charge of a situation
up the creek without a paddle	in a situation without having what you need to proceed in a productive or position manner
upside down	owe more on a loan or note than the item being financed is worth
uptown	very classy
useless as tits on a boar hog	a male pig would not need this anatomical structure for nursing its offspring

V [2]

vim and vigor	spunk and energy
voice like a foghorn	low and deep voice

W [129]

waddle like a duck	ducks waddle

waggin' his tail	acting happy and friendly
wait until the eleventh hour	wait until the last minute
waitin' for my ship to come in	waiting for a great chance of opportunity
waitin' for the second time around	waiting for a second chance
waitin' on him hand and foot	attending to someone or catering to their needs exclusively as a servant
wake up and smell the coffee	become realistic
walk in his shoes	put yourself in his place before you judge or condemn him
walk softly and carry a big stick	act more that deliver verbal threats
walkin' encyclopedia	has a lot of information and remembers details well
walkin' my legs off	walking a very long way
walkin' on eggs	being very careful guarded
walkin' the straight and narrow	followed the rules exactly
walkin' time bomb	ready to destruct at any moment
walks like a switchboard operator... all lines busy	the term refers to a very sexy moving woman. In the early days of telephony companies used manual telephone switchboards, and switchboard operators connected calls. They did this by inserting a pair of phone plugs into the appropriate jacks. These operators and system were gradually phased out and replaced by automated

systems allowing direct dialing within a local area and eventually long-distance and international direct dialing. My mother Ruby Jo Slaughter Slayden was a switchboard operator during WWII at Ft. Campbell Military Base in Kentucky which is about 20 minutes from Clarksville, Tennessee.

wanderlust — a strong desire to travel

war in the camp tonight — internal strife specifically between spouses in their home

warm as toast — warm and comfortable

washed my sins away — The Christian Bible speaks of our sins being washed away or it means we are forgiven by God through the grace of God through Christ.

washed-out blonde	a woman whose hair color has faded
waste not want not	to conserve something to not be in the need of it in the future
wasted	very tired either physically or emotionally
watchin' over her like a mother hen with one chick	being overprotective
water haul	a fruitless attempt or effort
water-logged	soaked with water
water off a duck's back	does not affect a person in the slightest
water over the dam	something that happened in the past and cannot be recalled or undone
water seeks its own level	people of quality and integrity seek out other people of quality and integrity and people of low quality and integrity seek out people of low quality and integrity
way off base	mistaken and incorrect about something
we'll cross that bridge when we get to it	we will react when something happens and not be insecure and fearful before something occurs
we've frogged our skins today	indicating that a person has overeaten likening them to the bullfrog who stretches his throat skin to croak
weak as a kitten	very weak

wear out your welcome   staying too long at someone's house until it becomes uncomfortable or an inconvenience

wear you out   a severe spanking

wearin' hand-me-downs   wearing clothes previous worn by someone else

wearin' his heart on his sleeve   too ready to be emotionally hurt

wearin' nothin' but a smile naked

weather setting in for a spell   the weather looks as if it will remain as it is for a considerable time

wee'uns we

welcome to the club   you are now experiencing what we have experienced

well for cryin' out loud   statement of amazement

well...holy cow   statement of exclamation of surprise

well...I'll be a suck egg mule   saying of disgust

well...kiss my foot   statement of dismay and dismissal

well-read educated

went over like a lead balloon   was not an accepted idea

went through his money like a dose of epson salts   Epson salts was used for constipation as a laxative

wet behind the ears   very inexperienced

wet blanket   a person who creates a negative situation or puts a damper on something causing everyone else to feel uncomfortable

wet your whistle   take a drink

what are you doin'...writin' a book...

leave that chapter out	you do not need to have that information
what are you lookin' at	a rhetorical and hostile question expressing discomfort of the person being looked or stared at?
what do you make of it	how do you explain or interpret it?
what drives the wagon	the impetus for something or cause for it happening
what is good for the goose is good for the gander	A goose is a female bird, and a gander is a male bird. Every individual person should be treated with equity.
what goes around comes around	if you do someone a wrong you can expect that at some point you will be wronged as well
what has come over you	what is responsible for your recent actions
what in tarnation	Noun. tarnation (countable and uncountable, plural tarnations) (archaic) The act or process of damnation or reprobation; hell. What in tarnation is going on? (obsolete)

Source: Wiktionary

what in the blue blazes	an exclamation used to emphasize surprise, shock, anger or disgust
"What in the Sam Hill"	The term Sam Hill is an American English slang phrase, a euphemism or minced oath for "the devil" or "hell"
what in the cat hair	exclamation of surprise and disapproval
what's your problem	what is wrong with you
what's got into you	what is wrong with you
what's the matter...cat got your tongue	The phrase "Cat Got Your Tongue" is used to describe when someone is at a loss of words or being unusually quiet.

The origin of the idiom 'cat got your tongue' is an intriguing one. Although many believe the "cat" in question is of the feline variety, it's the cat o' nine tails, a whip commonly used to flog sailors who misbehaved. On English sailing ships, anyone entrusted with a secret by a higher officer would be threatened with "the cat" for telling; thus, the saying 'has the cat got your tongue?' became slang for "are you afraid to tell?"

(Ati, 2021)

what-cha-ma-call-it	an item whose name has been forgotten or never known
what...you want egg in your beer	what more would you want than what you have
when it rains it pours	bad misfortune seems to all come at once
when pigs fly	never
when push comes to shove	when things accelerate, and you must act

when the cows come home

unpredictable and eventually but slowly

when the day of reckoning comes

the day of reckoning refers to the Last Judgment of God n Christian and Islamic belief during which everyone after death is called to account for their actions and can also simply mean a time at which someone's actions are discovered and that they are required to explain their actions

Source: Wikipedia

when the eagle flies

pay day

when you get to the end of your rope

when you desperately run out of options

when you were just a smile on your mother's face.

before you were born

where is my kick back

an inquiry about the kind of reward that can be expected as compensation for support

where were you when the lights went down

where were you when a particular event of importance happened can also imply that a person should have been aware of something that was occurring

while they're talkin' 'bout me they're givin' somebody else a rest

a gossip will eventually talk about everyone he or she knows giving others a reprieve

while you're gettin' a meal, I'll get a snack
a threat pending a fight

whirl wind affair
a fast and temporary love affair

whisperin' sweet nothin's in your ear
whispering sweet and complimentary conversation in a lover's ear

whistle britches
pants that rub together in the thigh area causing a swishing sound

whistle stop
a small train station at which a train makes regular stops

white as a ghost
very pale

whittle you down to my size
reduce you in a manner so that I can handle you

who asked you to put your two cents worth in
who asked for your very poor input

who in the world do you think you are
why do you think you are important in adding information or an opinion to this situation

whopper jawed
crooked or out of alignment

who pulled your chain
who asked you also implying that a person is a dog

whole lot of nothin'
absolutely nothing

whole ball of wax
the total or entirety of something

whoopin' and hollerin'	screaming in a lighthearted fashion or situation of levity
what's up	what is going on or what is happening
wide as it is long	all options are the same from any vantage point
wide place in the road	a very small town
wild as a buck	wild and freely acting in a promiscuous manner
wild as a coot	wild and freely acting in a promiscuous manner
wild eyes	eyes wide open with an alarmed facial expression
windin' road,	a road with many curves
wipe him out	do away with a person or exterminate them
wise as an owl	very wise especially in terms of advice
witch-hunt	A witch-hunt or a witch purge is a search for people who have been labelled "witches" or a search for evidence of witchcraft, and it often involves a moral panic or mass hysteria. The classical period of witch-hunts in Early Modern Europe and Colonial America took place in the Early Modern period or about 1450 to 1750.
with flying colors	Prior to the 18th century, a ship's appearance upon the immediate return to the port could communicate

how the crew fared at sea because modern communication devices did not exist. Ships that were victorious would sail into port with flags flying from the mastheads. A ship that had been defeated, if still afloat, would be forced to "strike her colors", or to take them down, signifying her defeat.

(Dictionary.com, 2021)

within ear shot	within hearing range
won't give an inch	will not budge on an opinion or decision
won't take a back seat to anyone	will not allow anyone to take precedence over them or go before them
won't take no for an answer	will not accept no
wood butcher	a carpenter
work yourself up into a dither	get upset and emotionally distraught
workin' for peanuts	working for little pay
workin' up a storm	working in a manner like a raging storm
workin' up a sweat	working in a manner to start perspiring due to the physical effort and exertion
workin' your fingers to the bone	working very hard and relentlessly
worn out	exhausted
worn to a frazzle	exhausted

worth his weight in gold	a worthy and trusted individual
worthless as a wooden nickel	worth absolutely nothing
wouldn't be caught dead wearin' that	would not wear that under any circumstances
wouldn't believe him on a stack of Bibles	person cannot be trusted to tell the truth as in swearing on the Bible in court or federal actions
wouldn't know the answer if it hit you in the face	person doesn't really know what is true even if confronted with the truth
wouldn't know the truth if you stepped in its	person doesn't really know what is true even if confronted with the truth
wouldn't touch that with a ten-foot pole	I don't want to get involved or take a position on that
wouldn't trust him as far as I could throw him	have no trust in this person
wound up	tense and emotionally upset
wound up the day	finished the day's events
wringin' wet	as wet as a cloth straight out of the wash tub on wash day
wrinkled as a stewed prune	very wrinkled
wrong as wrong can be	totally incorrect
wrong end of the stick	going about this all wrong
wrung out wet and hung out to dry	someone was deceived, framed, or convicted inappropriately and

without proper due process

X [0]

Y [61]

ya'll come	you all come to see us or come back to see us
'Ya ought a'	you should
yakety yak don't talk back	Don't talk back or argue with me or there will be repercussions. This saying comes from a popular song.

"Yakety Yak" is a song written, produced, and arranged by Jerry Leiber and Mike Stoller.

Yankee an individual originating north of the Mason-Dixon Line, originally the historical political boundary between Maryland and Pennsylvania in the United States in the pre-Civil War period. (Britannica.com, 2021)

yelling his lungs out	loudly yelling
you ain't just whistlin' Dixie	you are not joking
you ain't seen nothin' yet	you haven't seen what I am truly capable of yet
you ain't so sharp yourself	you aren't very smart and capable yourself
you and what army	how can you attain this alone or with who's help
you be the judge of that	you decide about something

you better walk a straight line — you had better have behavior above reproach

you can bet your top dollar — you can rest assured

you can't have a smooth ride on a buckin' horse — don't expect that something is going to be easy to attain if the circumstances surrounding you are difficult

you can't hoot with the owls and soar with the eagles — understand that others categorize or stereotype you according to those that you associate with

you can't make a silk purse out of a sow's ear — you are unable to turn something ugly or inferior into something attractive or of value as in no matter how expensive his clothes, he still looks sloppy.

you can't sell me the Brooklyn Bridge — you can't swindle or cheat me

you can't take it with you — worldly wealth will do you no good in Heaven

you catch more flies with honey than you do with vinegar — you can attain more being sweet and loving to others rather than harsh and sour

you don't know him from Adam's off ox — The phrase *doesn't know someone from Adam's off ox* means the speaker is not acquainted with the person, that the person is a stranger to him. An off ox is the draft animal in a team that is situated on the right, the farthest away from the driver. The driver places the most experienced draft animal closest to his guiding leads, hoping that the off ox will simply follow what the lead animal does. The off ox is not as prized as the near ox.

(Grammarist, 2021)

you don't know the half of it	you don't know the whole story
you don't know when the gettin's good	you don't know when to stop a behavior or action
you fouled it up	you did something completely incorrectly
you haven't lost a daughter…you've gained a son	you will always have your daughter when she marries and will also gain a son
you hit the nail on the head	you are exactly right which is the only way to drive a nail in to a piece of wood
you kids skoo-doodle	a direction to children to remove themselves from your company
you look like Ned in the first-grade reader to me	you look very immature or inexperienced

you made the bed...now lie in it	you are responsible for the conditions in the situation that you have created by your actions
you messed in your nest	you have made a mistake that affects you directly by your actions
you missed the boat	you have lost your opportunity
you must be out of your tree	you must not be thinking in a rational manner
you must have nose trouble	you are too curious about other's business and too nosy
you need not flare up	don't get upset in temperament
you need to wash your own dirty line.	you need to take care of your own problems and deficiencies
you need your head examined	you need help in reconsidering something because your judgment is not rational
you out did yourself	you really did an excellent job
you owe it to yourself	you should do this for yourself
you sound like a broken record	a broken vinyl or Victrola record skips and repeats itself as it plays on the player
you sound like a Victrola record	a broken vinyl or Victrola record skips and repeats itself as it plays on the player

you sound like an echo	I have heard what you are saying before
you think you're a big man	you are pretentious and overconfident
you turn me on	you are exciting to me
you turn my stomach	you upset me emotionally
you were knee-high to a grasshopper	you were a young small child
you will have to face the music	you are accountable for your actions
you'd argue with a fence post	you are argumentative with everyone about everything
you'll rue the day	you will see a time that you will be sorry
you're barkin' up the wrong tree	you are pursuing something from the wrong perspective
you're breedin' a scab on your nose	you are looking for a fight
you're cuttin' your nose off to spite your face	what you're doing will not help you but harm you
you're driving me to my grave	you are causing great anxiety and grief
you're durn tooten	you are correct
you're just asking for it	you are provoking someone's anger
you're just puttin' me on	you are surely joking me
you're just racin' your motor	trying to physically attract someone
you're lyin' through your teeth	you are telling a bold lie
you're runnin' on a downhill pull	moving quickly
you're so lucky if you fell in the water, you'd come up bone dry with a fish in each pocket	you seem to persevere in a positive manner regardless

of the conditions or
situation that you are in

**you're the one who brings home
the bacon**
the primary income earner

you'uns
collective pronoun for you

you've put a noose around your neck
 you have put yourself in a
state of jeopardy

**your eyes are bigger than
your stomach**
you are incapable of
consuming or using all that
you initially assume that
you can consume

Z [1]

Zots!
a saying my Great Aunt
Arlie May Baker Wilder
used when she pointed her
finger at a bee once and
exclaimed Zots! the bee
"fell dead"

References

A Jenny or Female Donkey. In Fort Worth Weekly (2021). Retrieved from https://www.google.com/search?q=Jenny+donkey+braying&tbm=isch& ved=2ahUKEwiF1ve58MP0AhXGYqwKHVvgD9oQ2- cCegQIABAA&oq=Jenny+donkey+braying&gs_lcp=CgNpbWcQA1AAWNE UYNoXaABwAHgAgAFaiAGbBJIBATeYAQCgAQGqAQtnd3Mtd2l6LWltZ8 ABAQ&sclient=img&ei=1hWoYYWTNcbFsQXbwL_QDQ&bih=1273&biw= 1093&client=safari&hl=en- US#imgrc=54_y9qaS_LROXM&imgdii=c2imudZ_Uc1TYM

Bad Penny. In the Free Dictionary by Farlex (2021). Retrieved from https://idioms.thefreedictionary.com/turn+up+like+a+bad+penny

Barber Pole In Wikimedia Commons retrieved from https://commons.wikimedia.org/wiki/File:Barber_pole_(manufactured_ by_the_Marvy_Company),_Minneapolis,_Minnesota_LCCN2017703862.tif

Barbers Shop. In the *Barbering Time Line* in the National Barber Museum and Hall of Fame (2021). Barbering Time Line. Retrieved from https://www.nationalbarbermuseum.org/about/barbering-timeline

Bee In Wiki Media Commons Retrieved from https://www.123rf.com/photo_46407058_dead-bee.html

Brass Balls. In grammar Monster (2021). What is the origin of the Saying "To Freeze the Balls Off a Brass Monkey". Retrieved from https://www.grammarmonster.com/sayings_proverbs/freeze_balls_off_ brass_monkey.htm

Bully Beef. In *Express (2021)*. The battle to feed Tommy: New exhibition looks at the diet of a WW1 soldier. Retrieved from https://www.express.co.uk/news/world-war-1/502452/The-Battle-to-feed-Tommy-The-diet-of-a-WW1-soldier

Carter Pills. In WebMD, Carter's Little Pills Tablet, Delayed Release (Enteric Coated)-Uses, Side Effects, and More. Retrieved from https://www.webmd.com/drugs/2/drug-2131/carters-little-pills-oral/details

Cat Got Your Tongue. In Ati. The Disturbing Literal Origins of the Phrase "Cat got Your Tongue?" Retrieved from https://allthatsinteresting.com/cat-got-your-tongue

Civil War Flags In Sutori Retrieved from https://www.sutori.com/en/story/civil-war-annotated-timeline--ApeZ7MqzZcjLNwRERinajG8Y

Coca-Cola. In The Coca-Cola Company (2021). Retrieved from https://www.coca-colacompany.com/company/history/the-birth-of-a-refreshing-idea

Cocklebur. In Britannia Encyclopedia (2021). Retrieved from https://www.britannica.com/plant/cocklebur

Cold Enough to Freeze the Balls off a Brass Monkey. In grammar Monster (2021). Retrieved from https://www.grammarmonster.com/sayings_proverbs/freeze_balls_off_brass_monkey.htm

Come Hell or High Water. In Google Dictionary (2021). Retrieved from https://www.google.com/search?q=come+hell+or+high+water&client=safari&channel=mac_bm&ei=vAypYdWAF7qyqtsPyq-mgAc&ved=0ahUKEwjVztX028X0AhU6mWoFHcqXCXAQ4dUDCA4&uact=5&oq=come+hell+or+high+water&gs_lcp=Cgdnd3Mtd2l6EAMyBQguEIAEMgUIABCABDIFCAAQgAQyBQgAEIAEMgUILhCABDIFCAAQgAQyBQgA

EIAEMgUIABCABDIFCAAQgAQyBQguEIAEOhQIABDqAhC0AhCKAxC3Ax
DUAxDlAjoECAAQQzoKCC4QxwEQowIQQzoICAAQgAQQsQM6DgguEIAE
ELEDEMcBEKMCOhEILhCABBCxAxCDARDHARDRAzoOCC4QgAQQsQMQ
xwEQ0QM6CggAELEDEIMBEEM6BAguEEM6BQgAEJECOgUILhCRAjoLCC
4QgAQQsQMQgwE6CwguEIAEEMcBEK8BOggILhCABBCxA0oECEEYAEo
FCEASATFQAFiQLmC2MWgBcAB4AIABjwGIAc4SkgEFMTEuMTKYAQCg
AQGwAQrAAQE&sclient=gws-wiz

Creamed Beef on Toast. In the Naval Historical Foundation (2021). In
Chow: Creamed Sliced Beef on Toast (S.O.S). Retrieved from
https://www.navyhistory.org/2016/04/chow-creamed-sliced-beef-on-
toast-s-o-s/

"God must have loved the poor because He made so many of them". In
English Language and Usage (2021). Retrieved from
https://english.stackexchange.com/questions/535688/origin-of-the-
saying-god-must-love-the-poor-because-he-made-so-many-of-them

Got More Money Than Carter Has Pills. In the Free Dictionary. (2021).
Retrieved from
https://idioms.thefreedictionary.com/more+than+Carter+has+pills

"Great Scott". In Mental Floss, "Who's the 'Scott' in Great Scott?" (2021).
Retrieved from
https://www.mentalfloss.com/article/624303/great-scott-expression-
origin

Heel Toe Shifting. In Track Days. "What is Heel Toe Shifting?" (2021).
Retrieved from
https://www.trackdays.co.uk/news/tutorial-on-what-is-heel-toe-
shifting/

I Won't Kowtow for Anyone. In Google Dictionary. (2021). Retrieved from
https://www.google.com/search?q=kowtow&client=safari&channel=ma
c_bm&ei=LRCpYZurLMynqtsPtrqhuAI&ved=0ahUKEwjb9faY38X0AhXM
k2oFHTZdCCcQ4dUDCA4&uact=5&oq=kowtow&gs_lcp=Cgdnd3Mtd2l6E

AMyCAgAELEDEJECMggIABCxAxCRAjIICAAQgAQQsQMyBQgAEIAEMgUI
ABCABDIFCAAQgAQyBQgAEIAEMgUIABCABDIFCAAQgAQyBQgAEIAEOg
oIABDqAhC0AhBDOhAILhDHARDRAxDqAhC0AhBDOgUIABCRAjoICC4Q
gAQQsQM6EQguEIAEELEDEIMBEMcBEKMCOg4ILhCABBCxAxDHARDRA
zoOCC4QgAQQsQMQxwEQowI6BAgAEEM6EAguELEDEIMBEMcBEKMCE
EM6BwguELEDEEM6BAguEEM6DQguEIAEEMcBEKMCEAo6BwguEIAEE
ApKBAhBGABQAFiCFWD1F2gBcAB4AIABcIgBwQSSAQM0LjKYAQCgAQG
wAQrAAQE&sclient=gws-wiz

In A Pig's Eye. In Collins. (2021). Retrieved from
https://www.collinsdictionary.com/us/dictionary/english/in-a-pigs-eye

Indian Giver. In Urban Dictionary. Retrieved from
https://www.urbandictionary.com/define.php?term=Indian-Giver

It's Close Enough for Government Work. In (Wiktionary, 2021). Retrieved
from
https://en.wiktionary.org/wiki/close_enough_for_government_work

It's Your Dime. In Urban Dictionary, 2021). Retrieved from
https://en.wiktionary.org/wiki/close_enough_for_government_work

I won't kowtow to anyone. In Urban Dictionary (2021). Retrieved from
https://www.urbandictionary.com/define.php?term=kowtow

Jury-Rigged. In Dictionary.com. (2021). Retrieved from
https://www.dictionary.com/browse/jury-rigged

Methuselah. In Christianity. (2021). Retrieved from
https://www.christianity.com/wiki/people/who-was-methuselah-in-
the-bible.html

Nice Nasty. In Urban Dictionary. (2021). Retrieved from
https://www.urbandictionary.com/define.php?term=Nice-nasty

Photographs of Geoffrey Scott Baker. (ca 2021). Geoffrey Scott Baker. www. OellaWorks.com. In
https://gsbphotography.photoshelter.com/image/I0000NN2pPF6z_6s

Saturday Night Special In Wikimedia Commons Retrieved from https://commons.wikimedia.org/wiki/File:R%C3%B6hm_RG-14_Reagan_attempted_assassination_gun.jpg

Saw Briars. Photograph by Geoffrey Barker (2021). Retrieved from https://www.google.com/search?q=saw+briars&client=safari&rls=en&source=lnms&tbm=isch&sa=X&ved=2ahUKEwimzd3T8cP0AhXwl2oFHRG5CFQQ_AUoAXoECBMQAw&biw=1093&bih=1273&dpr=2#imgrc=Ao1aD2keDq4-MM

Sick As A Dog. In The Idioms: Largest Idioms Dictionary. (2021). Retrieved from http://www.the idioms.com/?s=sick+as+a+dog

Sloan's Liniment. In Drugs.com (2021). Retrieved from https://www.drugs.com/mtm/sloan-s-liniment.html

Snake Oil. In The Tribune. (2021). Retrieved from https://www.sanluisobispo.com/news/local/news-columns-blogs/phc

Soup Kitchen. In U-S-History.com (2021). Retrieved from https://www.u-s-history.com/pages/h1660.html

Step-ins. In Museum of London. (2021). Retrieved from http://deargolden.blogspot.com/2011/07/1920s-lingerie-step-in.html

Strike while the Iron is Hot. In Google Dictionary (2021). Retrieved from http://chrome.google.com/webstore/detail/google-dictionary-by-google

Telephone Operators In Wikipedia Commons Retrieved from https://commons.wikimedia.org/wiki/File:Telephone_operators,_1952.jpg

Turn Up Like a Bad Penny. In The Free Dictionary by Farlex. (2021) Retrieved from https://www.thefreedictionary.com

With Flying Colors. In Dictionary.com. (2021) Retrieved from https://www.dictionary.com/browse/flying-colors

Yankee. In Britannica.com. (2021). Retrieved from https://www.britannica.com/search?query-Yankee

You Don't Know Him From Adam's Off Ox. In Grammarist. (2021) Retrieved from
https://grammarist.com/idiom/adams-off-ox/

CPSIA information can be obtained
at www.ICGtesting.com
Printed in the USA
BVHW091752260822
645588BV00001B/104